TONGUES

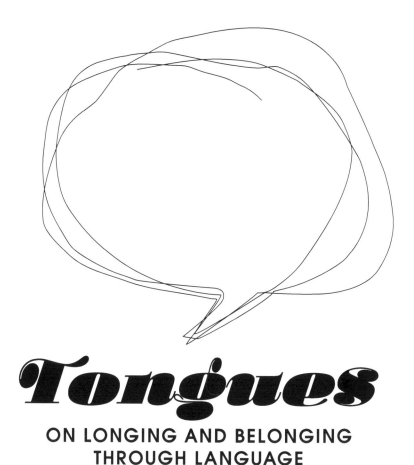

Tongues

ON LONGING AND BELONGING
THROUGH LANGUAGE

edited by Eufemia Fantetti,
Leonarda Carranza, and Ayelet Tsabari

Essais Series No. 12

Book*hug Press
TORONTO

Library and Archives Canada Cataloguing in Publication

Title: Tongues : on longing and belonging through language / edited by Leonarda
    Carranza, Eufemia Fantetti, and Ayelet Tsabari.
Other titles: Tongues (2021)
Names: Carranza, Leonarda, editor. | Fantetti, Eufemia, 1969- editor. | Tsabari,
    Ayelet, 1973- editor.
Series: Essais (Toronto, Ont.) ; no. 12.
Description: First edition. | Series statement: Essais series ; no. 12
Identifiers: Canadiana (print) 20210279354 | Canadiana (ebook) 20210280093
    ISBN 9781771667142 (softcover)
    ISBN 9781771667159 (EPUB)
    ISBN 9781771667166 (PDF)
Subjects: LCSH: Sociolinguistics. | LCSH: Identity (Psychology) | LCSH: Native language.
    | LCSH: Language acquisition.
Classification: LCC P40 .T66 2021 | DDC 306.44—dc23

The production of this book was made possible through the generous assistance of
the Canada Council for the Arts and the Ontario Arts Council. Book*hug Press also
acknowledges the support of the Government of Canada through the Canada Book
Fund and the Government of Ontario through the Ontario Book Publishing Tax
Credit and the Ontario Book Fund.

Book*hug Press acknowledges that the land on which we operate is the traditional
territory of many nations, including the Mississaugas of the Credit, the Anishnabeg,
the Chippewa, the Haudenosaunee, and the Wendat peoples. We recognize the
enduring presence of many diverse First Nations, Inuit, and Métis peoples and are
grateful for the opportunity to meet, work, and learn on this territory.

CONTENTS

INTRODUCTION

TONGUES **IS A** book we dreamt up together, both separately and collectively. At some point or another, two of us walked down a wintry Toronto street speaking of a book just like this one. At another point, maybe in the spring, one of us called another to discuss how this idea could become reality. As immigrants and daughters of immigrants, as racialized women, as writers who lost their mother tongues or their ancestral languages, as English-as-a-second-language learners, we share a curiosity and passion about language.

We had the unique opportunity to work on this collection of essays during a pandemic. As the world went into isolation, cities locked down, and people were told to stay apart, we had the honour of inviting twenty-three distinct voices who shared our fascination and love of language to join this conversation. Essays arrived throughout the summer and into the fall—and as our lives shrunk and a restricted world became the new normal, the collection grew in breadth and scope. The essays bridged the distance, anchored and moved us, and eased our loneliness, much like language itself can do. We were reminded of Kai Cheng Thom's essay where she defines language as "the fluid within the collective body: like plasma, like blood, like spinal fluid, it carries nutrients and information from one unit to the next."

Personal, lyrical, and candid, the essays in this collection investigate the intimate relationship between identity and language, confront the pain of losing a mother tongue or an ancestral language, and celebrate the joys and empowerment that come with reclamation. "I use Anishinaabemowin in my work as a way to reclaim my culture, for just as Cedar is rooted in the earth, so my culture is rooted in the language," writes Ashley Hynd in her essay, "The Seven Grandfathers and Translation." Others admit to purposely unlearning their mother tongue as an act of survival. As Kamal Al-Solaylee writes in "Tongue-Tied," forgetting Arabic was "part of a journey of self-reinvention."

We envisioned an anthology that would celebrate the richness and aliveness of Canada's language diversity. There are more than seventy Indigenous languages and over two hundred mother tongues spoken in Canada. Some 7.4 million Canadians speak French, and 5.8 million Canadians speak at least two languages at home. Yet the irony of this project was not lost on us. Here we were editing an anthology about language written in one language and one language only, "the winner's English," Melissa Bull calls it in her essay, "English Baby."

The legacy of colonialism is not ignored in these pages, as writers hold English and its colonial violence to account. The contributors to this anthology challenge us to think about the intricate relationship between English and privilege, and how power affects language learning, specifically the experience of learning English in Canada—a predominantly white, settler, colonial nation—and the shame and exclusion that often come with second-language learning. They demand that we think deeply about the languages we acquire, the languages we lose, the ones that are taken from us, and the ones we fight and struggle to reclaim. These essays are transformative. They confront us with the exclusionary, daily violence of racist, ableist, and cis-normative language. In "It's Just a Figure of Speech," Amanda Leduc asks us to consider our complicity with ableist language and how it "reinforces the idea that there is only one way to be in the world." In "Gender Fluent," Logan Broeckaert reflects on how gendered language affects the way we see ourselves and our place in the world, and in "What Are You? A Field Study," Rowan McCandless magnifies the way that white supremacy and othering appear in everyday talk.

While the scope of this project was such that it didn't allow for translated works to be included, we hope the many languages that make an appearance throughout the various texts pay tribute to the multilingual Canada we know. We hope they inspire readers to think more deeply about the act of italicizing (a choice of marking "foreign" language in texts, which Rebecca Fisseha examines at length in her essay, "Say Something in Your Language") and its relationship to othering. As for when to italicize, we allowed the writers to make their own choices on the matter.

Welcome to a series of profound, compelling personal narratives that explore the interrelationship between language, power, and privilege. As editors and writers, we invite you to join in and share our curiosity about the multiple ways that language lives and breathes inside each of us.

Eufemia Fantetti
Leonarda Carranza
Ayelet Tsabari

Kamal Al-Solaylee

TONGUE-TIED

The sound of silence is a precious commodity on the streets of Cairo, a city where the official soundtrack might as well be a symphony of car horns and shouting matches among a population pushed to the edge by income inequality and political corruption. And yet, in all the taxi and Uber rides I shared with my Cairo-based older sister, Farida, during a visit in 2019, I was instructed to remain silent. If I talk, she warned me, the driver might recognize my broken, foreign-sounding Arabic and try to scam us. She'll give directions, negotiate fare, and handle any small talk, which at times was anything but. No two Egyptians can share a small space without getting into an argument about the direction of this once-hospitable and safe country. (Hint: wrong direction.)

I welcomed being quiet, invisible even, for a few minutes or, depending on Cairo traffic, an hour or two. Machismo is a default male behaviour in much of this city, so I loved seeing my sister in full command mode while I sat pretty.

The many silent rides over my two-week visit helped me process something I've been struggling to vocalize for years.

I'm a native Arabic speaker who spent fifteen formative years of my life in Cairo with my Yemeni family. I excelled in that language's complex grammar, picked up from a generation of Arabic schoolteachers now long dead, and mastered its local variation. When I was a teen, no one could tell I wasn't born in Cairo or that my parents and older siblings spoke a different dialect at home. I spent my childhood consuming a steady diet of Egyptian films and television dramas that made my own parents' Yemeni accents sound unsophisticated—what Egyptians would call *falahi*, or peasant-like. My middle-class Egyptian friends called their parents mama and baba. At home my siblings and I used the more Bedouin-inflected *oma* or *aba*. I longed to be like other Cairenes I knew, and I pretty much sounded like one whenever I wasn't at home.

And yet here I was, thirty-three years since I had last lived in Cairo, stumbling to finish a sentence at the airport with customs officers or to order off the menu in restaurants. Silence became me. I felt so uncomfortable speaking English in an Arabic setting, and self-conscious enough about my Arabic, that keeping quiet seemed like the safest option. Looking back, I can't blame the state of being a stranger in my own land on external factors. I'm the one who silenced my voice and had actively eroded my command of and access to Arabic through a decades-long process I'm only now beginning to understand. Arabic was my birthright. How did I squander what came so naturally to me? Can I still claim an identity as an Arab when I'm stumped by the very thing that defines it: the language my people speak?

LINGUISTS REFER TO the phenomenon of losing native tongues as first-language attrition, or FLA, a process that happens when people are isolated from other speakers of that language or when another language dominates. The term *mother tongue* has always implied an umbilical connection to the languages we first learn at home, a fixed identity based on the language you heard the most as an infant. Recent research suggests that, by their first year, infants can distinguish between their parents' language and other languages. In a world where nearly 260 million people do not live in their country of birth and mostly function in a second language, studies of FLA are gaining momentum and testing what we know about how we acquire, use, and lose what is most native to us.

This welcome body of research brings both comfort and understanding for those of us "suffering" from FLA—at least on an intellectual or theoretical level. There's a sense of relief in learning that our "condition" has a name; that what I've come to regard as a personal and private shift is being studied by linguists and psychologists. Look, *oma*, I'm in a textbook!

Theory and practice, however, sometimes connect and oftentimes diverge. The contours of my own experience of losing Arabic don't always fit into existing research, which, by and large, views FLA as a naturally occurring phenomenon—something that happens with time and acculturation—and mainly dwells on younger learners. If I want to understand why I remained silent during the cab rides in Cairo, or why I excused myself from some tense family discussions on my rare visits to Yemen, I need to retrace the steps that led to where I am today: someone who writes, thinks, and dreams in a language different from the one he was born into.

MY DERELICTION OF Arabic was a conscientious move and part of a journey of self-reinvention I embarked on in my late teens. The *Quran*, the holy book of the Muslim faith in which I was born, is written in Arabic. As I was coming out as a gay man in the early 1980s and reading up on sexual liberation, I needed distance from both the religion and its official text that, I felt, vilified my desires.

English became more than a second language; it drew a personalized road map to freedom, dignity, and sex.

I didn't see being gay as an experience that could unfold in Arabic. The language lacked the vocabulary and textual resources to help me accept who I am, who I choose to love or fuck. If anything, it mobilized hate and discrimination against homosexuality, which only appeared in literature and popular arts as a sin or a Western affliction. The only Arabic word for it while growing up was either *shaz*, which meant abnormal, or *Looty*, a reference to Lot, Abraham's nephew, of Sodom and Gomorrah.

English, on the other hand, had it all figured out. What could be lovelier than the word *gay* to describe how I felt about myself. Happiness and a joie de vivre lie at its roots. And what's more aspirational than the gay liberation movement, by then more than a decade in progress? Not even the advent of AIDS around the same time could dull my interest in English as a gay language. The connection between gay men and what was then a deadly disease doubled my access to reading material on my sexuality in Cairo of the early to mid-1980s. Many years later, several LGBT rights activists in the Middle East would point out that AIDS-prevention work allowed them a window to broach sexual rights and support for the queer community. The more neutral-sounding word *methaly*, or *same*, to refer to gay men in particular, grew out of this new health-focused context.

From the time I was about nineteen, I made it a point to stop reading or listening to Arabic, to speak it only when necessary and to upgrade English from second to first language—a process that became more immersive when I moved to England at twenty-four to study literature, eventually earning a PhD in Victorian fiction. Such was my complete adoption of English that I turned down suggestions by potential doctoral supervisors to work on "colonial" literature— Richard Burton's translation of *Arabian Nights* or Lawrence Durrell's *Alexandria Quartet* were often suggested—and pursued such authors as

Charles Dickens and Wilkie Collins who were more "purely" English. Arabic language or settings meant contamination, a corruption of my resolve to exile myself from my native tongue and homeland.

All along, I picked up, quite naturally and through exposure to mostly native speakers, a refined English accent, which made me sound, if not posh, then at least educated and middle class in a country defined by class politics and resentments. With each graduate seminar, dinner party, or visit to a gay club, I drifted further away from the world of my mother, an illiterate shepherdess, and my father, a self-made businessman and anglophile whose own command of English had deteriorated once he stopped using it for work. His fate will not be mine.

I rewired my brain to think, speak, and write in one language, burying Arabic deep in the recesses of my mind. I didn't think of my plans as an elaborate artifice or a makeover, but as a means of countervailing my birth identity and establishing a real, new self. This is the me I deserved. There can be no sexual liberation if the language that oppressed me (and the society and family that spoke it) still lived within me and came out of my mouth. I even took classes in German and Spanish just to keep my native language further at bay. I cancelled my culture before cancel culture became a thing (or a right-wing false alarm).

Years later, while visiting my friend Guillermo in the Basque region of Spain—where the local Euskera language is under threat from Spanish—we got into an argument about our relationships with our mother tongues. We're both gay men of the same vintage. His family accepted his sexuality; mine wouldn't. He could live and love in his native tongue; I couldn't. More to the point, as the number of Euskera speakers dwindled in Spain, the one for Arabic speakers rose alongside the much higher birth rates in the region. Intellectually and politically, I could afford to lose Arabic because I knew the language wouldn't die with me. For a minority, any minority, the loss of language equals a loss of a way of life, of their very existence. Extinction begins when a language disappears. I found comfort in (and an excuse for) my attrition of Arabic, when looked at in this wider context. Egypt's population more than doubled between the time I left it (in 1986) and my last visit (2019): from 50.5 million to nearly 103 million. For every person who abandons Arabic, hundreds of thousands more are born into it.

I'd be lying if I didn't confess to a certain jealousy of the way Guillermo talked effortlessly to his parents and childhood friends.

IN 1998, AND AFTER two long-term relationships with men whose first languages were English and German, I met and fell in love with Motaz, a Canadian of Syrian background—who, like me, grew up as a native Arabic speaker. I had been living in Toronto for two and a half years by the time we met, and with the PhD completed and a new life beginning, one thing remained unchanged: my resolve not to speak Arabic. I hadn't factored in meeting an Arab gay man.

I don't believe we ever made a conscious decision or settled the matter over a conversation, but we rarely if ever used Arabic to discuss our relationship. We saved it for ordering food in Lebanese restaurants (so we could get the real stuff and not the watered-down versions they sell to white people) and to tease each other. As he was a modern dancer, I'd call him *Rakasa*—the term Egyptians use, often in a derogatory tone, for belly dancers. To him, I was a *hakawati*, a reference to the storyteller figure in Arabic folklore. This lasted for nearly five years. I speak for both of us when I say that we felt that Arabic would curse our relationship, destroying what we've built for ourselves. We needed to shield ourselves from the homophobia of our shared culture. That much worked out. Our relationship ended for other reasons.

Two more decades in Canada followed and, before I realized it, my Arabic had atrophied to the point where talking to my own family who live in Yemen about anything beyond their general welfare became a chore. Before every call, I'd brace myself for the awkwardness that followed. I try, but my vocabulary can't sustain a deep conversation about their emotional well-being, their frustrations, dreams, sorrows.

By the time the war in Yemen started in 2015, and we had to discuss such possibilities as staying alive, claiming refugee status in Egypt, sheltering from air strikes, or selling family assets to survive financially, my damaged Arabic probably made things worse. Who needs a tortured phone conversation with a sibling living in Canada when there's enough pain and suffering in their immediate world? I've abandoned them physically by studying in England and then immigrating to Canada, and psychologically by willing the native tongue that once bound us to atrophy. When they speak of it, my siblings view my transition into English as a combination of self-loathing and a rebellion that has outlasted my younger years. As they became more religious, they started to see my dereliction of Arabic as *haram*. My sister Hoda reads the *Quran* several times a year, a ritual she has maintained for almost two decades. Imagine her disappointment when I told her I didn't own a copy and, even if I did, I probably couldn't read it now. She said she'd pray for me.

As the war intensified over the last two years, so has my desire to reconnect with my family. My material condition and theirs may never match, but Arabic can at least bring us closer, making up for some of the lost decades apart. The first step in this journey is to reclaim my Arabic. Can we actually relearn our own native tongue? What would that look like?

As I pondered these questions, I came across the work of Chinese-American author Yiyun Li, who compares the process of erasing all traces of her Chinese to her two attempts at suicide. "My abandonment of my first language is personal, so deeply personal that I resist any interpretation—political or historical or ethnographical," she wrote in an essay for the *New Yorker*. "One's relationship with the native language is similar to that with the past. Rarely does a story start where we wish it had, or end where we wish it would."

With hindsight, I wonder about Li's highly personal view of language loss. I wanted to lose Arabic for reasons that relate to sexual politics. I wish to regain it, in part, also because of politics: national politics. As a person of colour witnessing the rise of populism and a return to fascist politics in the West—"Go back to where you came from" may become more than an angry chant from Trump supporters—I'm feeling less secure, less at home, in Canada than ever before. My concerns range from considering living in a place where people who look like me are the majority (the Middle East) to being forced to leave as part of some kind of ethnic rebalancing like the one happening in the United States. I don't think I'm being paranoid, even though I often am about other things.

Bill C-24 in Canada, which became a law in 2014, creates a two-tier citizenship: one for native-born Canadians and another for naturalized people like me. The law, introduced by the Conservative government of Stephen Harper, makes it easier for the government to strip some Canadians of their citizenship if they're deemed to constitute a national threat or if they've obtained it by fraud. Neither is applicable to me, but abuse of law comes naturally when racial anxieties and fascism enter the picture.

The possibility of losing my place in Canada, and by extension not living in the only language I master, shook me to the core. It unravelled what I spent decades stitching. It also underlined a particular case of imposter syndrome I've been keeping on the down low. My continuing erasure of Arabic after coming to Canada happened simultaneously with my expanding portfolio as a commentator on the Arab world and Muslim culture, a role I took on in part out of necessity but also out of career ambition as a journalist and author. Perhaps imposter syndrome is not the exact phrase here. How about ethnic fraud? I never hid my struggles with Arabic in my books but I certainly claimed more access to the culture and the people than I had a right to, given my inability to grasp the written parts of it in particular.

MY RETURN PASSAGE to my mother tongue has been a disorienting and at times humiliating experience. To do it properly, I started with some online "Arabic for Beginners" resources, which took me further back into my childhood than I was willing to go. I fared better with mid-level Arabic but found it too easy. What I wanted to regain most of all was the ease and comfort of colloquial Arabic (which by definition means Egyptian dialect for me), the kind of natural speech rhythm that my Basque friend takes for granted. I raided YouTube for movies from what has come to be known as the Beautiful Time (a belle époque of Egyptian and Lebanese film and music from the 1940s to the 1970s).

I can't begin to explain the sense of loss I experienced with every viewing of an old Egyptian movie. How did I deny myself access to such a treasure trove of wisecracking, melodramatic, break-into-songs-every-five-minutes back catalogue? The camp value and the homoerotic subtexts of male bonding alone sustained me for hours. And let me tell you: the young Omar Sharif is otherworldly beautiful. Slowly I began to feel comfortable singing along to the musical numbers, starting with the more popular ones of Shadia and Farid al-Atrash and graduating to the classical Arabic of select songs from Mohamed Abdel Wahab and Umm Kulthum, the two pillars of Arabic music in the twentieth century. I still don't understand what I'm singing along to at times, but since I do it mostly in the kitchen, I can get away with mouthing the words. I tried to read the first part of the *Cairo Trilogy* by Naguib Mahfouz, the Egyptian Nobel Prize–winning novelist, in Arabic, but that proved too advanced. Reading and writing Arabic will have to wait.

With nothing but popular film and music as preparation, I decided to plunge myself back into Cairo and see if retracing the geography of my childhood home might actually speed up the retrieval of Arabic. I believed the language was lurking just in the back of my mind; all it needed to restore itself to its former glory was a literal trip down memory lane.

The experiment worked in some contexts and backfired in others. My comprehension has improved but my spoken Arabic remains frozen in time. Colloquial Egyptian has moved on. When I tried to speak it with my sister and her children, they laughed it off because I sounded like a matinee idol from the movies I used to restore my Arabic. I relied on phrases and sentence structures that people in Cairo, even ones my age or older, no longer use. Think of someone coming to Toronto and talking like Cary Grant. As Li predicted, this story with language didn't end where I hoped it would: a triumphant return of the prodigal son. After one too many barbs about my dated Arabic, I decided to talk less and listen more. The practice of Arabic I wanted so much came at too high a price.

IT TOOK MORE than three decades for me to unlearn Arabic, so I shouldn't be surprised that regaining it requires more time and effort than I had anticipated. The teenage me in Cairo would have liked the tongue-tied man I became, as it would have signalled once and for all my elevation of English into a first language. The middle-aged Canadian feels more sombre about it.

I vacillate between thinking that regaining my command of Arabic could still happen and accepting that my relationship with my native tongue is better expressed in terms of mourning an impending death. My Arabic is on life support, and the odds are against it. Even if it were to be revived, through a miracle cure or hard work, it may never feel the same again. I'm not talking about the "You can never go home" feeling, but the fact that I can try as much as I want to build a bridge back to my language, my family, my part of the world, but will they take me back? Haven't they also moved on? In my mind, regaining a forgotten language has always been a drama in which I was a leading man and my family the supporting cast. It feels more and more like a one-person show, a one-sided expression of longing and memory.

Most of us with FLA can dream of returns to homelands and native tongues, but we can't count on welcome mats, even if we regain fluency. Not everything that's broken should be fixed. It's more realistic to expect us to step on the tiny pieces that have splintered, I tell myself. In English, of course. I have no idea, and may never do, how to express that thought in any other language.

Jenny Heijun Wills

A BIRD IN MY HANDS

reunited with my Korean family when I was an adult. I was born in Seoul. I was sent away. I was raised in Ontario, Canada. The English-speaking part. My husband is from Quebec. The French-only part. We live in Manitoba.

My Korean mother doesn't speak English. I understand very little Korean. We still try. We're still trying.

I can't pronounce my husband's name.
That's okay.

For years I couldn't pronounce my own name either.

An electrician came to the house once and, filling out the paperwork after he'd finished his task, pointed his pen at me and said, "I thought yours would be the difficult one."

People say my name is difficult to pronounce. I think my name sounds sexy. Like a sigh. If you're saying it properly, it makes your tongue go just the right amount of soft.

Only once has someone said my Korean name while kissing me. It startled me into opening my eyes.

They ask, "Spell it out," but are annoyed by the alphabet I use. They say, "Spell it in English," but I can't.
Those immigration officers tried decades ago but they wrecked it.

They ask me to say my name again and again until it stops making sense. Until it sounds ugly again.

Our girls laugh at my middle name, not caring that it was gifted to honour my Canadian grandmother and her chosen name. She too had been born with another name she didn't use. Though her reinvention was her choice. They laugh at the whiteness of my name, and I let them, even though I loved my grandmother very much.

As a small girl, I hid from schoolmates my broken Korean name, split in two syllables and buried near the end anyhow.

When the marriage certificate arrived, I feared there'd been a mistake. I didn't know about French Canadian baptismal names.

I anticipate the confusion of my name carved, one day, into a granite slab. The audacity of its length. The inaccuracy of its translation. I wonder if there will be someone caring enough to insist on Hangul for the right parts.

The Last time I was in Korea, I scanned my Korean grandfather's tomb, trying to learn his name. I never did. The text is too dense. I can't decipher name from place from clichéd Buddhist verse about existence.

•

Together, we took classes in tae kwon do. I was the only Korean there. I flinched each time we counted to ten as a group. The other students didn't care that the noises they made were just sounds. They also told me I was bowing wrong.

When I say, "Korean adoptee," I say it with a Midwest accent because the Minnesotans are the ones who talk the most, the loudest, the longest. I ponder the shape of vowels in our mouths when we have no one with whom to practise the words meant to describe us.

My Korean mother says the same phrase each time we speak on the phone. I think she asks how I'm doing. My response is always, I don't understand.

"Mulahyo" curls off the tip of my tongue like a bird call.
Over and over and over again.

I'll never know what my Korean mother's accent tells others about her. I can't tell if my father had a similar accent. I suspect not.

I'm afraid that my book will be translated into Hangul. I'm also worried it won't be.

What's the word for when your heart is racing but your body is calm?

When I'm in K-town, or better yet, Seoul, and I'm surrounded by those letters and sounds, my body blows open with desire.

In Korea, a woman yelled at me on the metro because I was speaking English to another adopted person. She thought we were flaunting our wealth, our education, our cosmopolitanism. A stranger on the train translated her anger for us.

My friend was from Denmark, where they learn to speak English, so she says, because American movies are rarely translated into Danish.

That day on the metro was like so many others. We laughed because we didn't know what else to do.

I told my Canadian parents once that I couldn't read the sign they pointed to because the words were written in Chinese. "How should we know?" they asked.

Family members accuse me often of twisting their words. Of listening too carefully to what is said and then speaking back. But what are words and language if not twisted already?

The first time I studied Korean was at the university. The instructor used analogies to Mandarin. All the other students were Chinese. They thought I was weird being Korean and having to learn to speak Korean.

My Canadian father held up flash cards so I could study for my exam.

My Korean sister is angry that I don't study Korean anymore. What she doesn't understand is that each time I fail I feel like I can't breathe.

A reviewer comments that she doesn't like my memoir because she's angered I didn't try harder to learn

Korean. It's not that studying this language is a challenge. It's that studying this language is like pressing a finger into the centre of yesterday's still-soft bruise.

Wise people tell me that language is integral to identity. But I've given up. So what now?

•

He says, "When we speak on the phone, you have the accent of an Asian girl from Southern Ontario raised by white people."
He tells me often.

He says, "When she speaks French, her accent is from a region of Quebec she's never seen."
He tells others often.

I can't make *that* sound in my throat. I can't roll my *r*'s. So I can't pronounce his name.

He says, "You anglos pronounce *r* like it's a vowel." He doesn't comment on how Koreans do it the same way French Canadians do.

He's smart.

•

I call her Unni because it is as if she is my older sister. She calls me Unni because it is as if I am hers.

•

My business cards state that I teach in the English Language Program at the university even though I told them many times it's Literary Studies. Something doesn't register.

Sometimes in Vancouver or Toronto or New York or San Francisco I enunciate more.
When I notice, I'm ashamed.

A man I once knew laughed when I said I taught English because he thought I was joking. "How can a Korean teach English?" he wondered. I didn't answer. But I locked eyes with his Asian wife. Then we both looked away.

When I teach that one book in translation, the students are surprised to learn that the original language was French. They expect something more exotic. They don't know anything about Bill 101.

The books I read sometimes talk about living between languages. The characters seem sad or stressed or unanchored.
    I don't live between languages, at least not the ones I desire.
    And that makes me sad and stressed and unanchored.

•

I barely remember a single word my Korean father ever said to me. But in the back of my mind is the heft of his laugh. The way he could make his voice so soft and, like that, lull me into letting down my guard. Even without words, I remember the baritone that fooled my mother first and then me.

Someone asked, "Do you ever dream in Korean?" No. I never do.

•

He says, "I'm losing my French." Sometimes this makes him frustrated. Sometimes this makes him laugh. I wonder at the slow forfeiture of language. It confuses me.

My Korean grandmother has Alzheimer's.
She's losing her tongue.
    Again.

I have to guess at my halmoni's age because I don't know how to ask. But let's say she was born in the late 1920s or early 1930s. I suppose she too had our language thieved from her mouth in infancy. I think of that writer I love who described the colonial violence that forced Koreans to live as Japanese and speak our own language only in twilight. Only in the dark.

I wonder if Halmoni had a different name back then. If she was remade, like me, one day one girl and the next, someone new. Did she feel relief or fear or something else when Korean was no longer outlawed?

(I've met many Japanese Canadians in Manitoba who also yearn for their ancestors' language. It's curious, sharing that loss.)

Now that everything is spilling through her fingers, what language occupies Halmoni's thoughts? In what language does she dream? The breathy, lilting titter of her girlhood or the wet, throaty rasp of the rest of her life?

To my unfamiliar ear, Korean is spoken not with the mouth but something deep down in the body. It erupts from the hot, gummy hollow where the collarbones meet, or maybe even somewhere lower, and is thick with resistance masked as another, unnameable thing.

She tells me the same story again and again. I catch a few words and hold them to my chest, fireflies in a jar. Her eyes, her back, are so tired I think she's fallen asleep. But she's awake. I pull "pretty baby" from a long line of unknowable words. Sounds, really. She knows I don't understand, but that's fine with her. At her age, there's no time for patience. She laughs, flashing a row of false teeth.

An article I read said that Alzheimer's has a genetic component. If I inherit, will words escape me too? Who will be there to explain to me why my insides and outsides don't match? Or what if no one believes me?

•

I try to imagine how many syllables the word *Alzheimer's* has in Korean. Five? Six?

When we were kids, we'd add the suffix –*er* to an English word and hope to fly under the radar in French class. These days, I break words into minuscule syllables and sometimes it works. Sometimes I can speak Korean. But then my Korean mother thinks I've magically learned our language, so I have to disappoint her all over again.

He can speak English until around 11:00 p.m. I can speak French until nine. This means our household is decidedly anglophone.

The girls laugh at how he says "air conditioner" when he means "hair conditioner" and vice versa. I let them. Just this once.

His voice drops a bit when he speaks in the voice that is expected of him. It turns me on. But I know it's all an act. Still, I eat it up.

•

In French there is no distinction between *to love* and *to like.*

•

My Korean sister watched reruns of *Friends* when she was learning to speak English. Could that be any more problematic?

When I lived in Korea, we developed a language of hand gestures and symbols to communicate. I still remember how we'd sign, "I'm hungry."

Once, I called my Korean mother on video chat when my heart was breaking. I couldn't explain why I was crying. So she just watched me cry. I wonder what she was thinking. I'm sorry to worry her like that. But I didn't know what else to do.

Korean is a bird in my hands. It wants out because it's not mine to hold.
    It's so breakable.
I'm afraid to kill it so I loosen my grip and it escapes me.

Karen McBride

PIMASHKOGOSI: CATCHING LANGUAGE

Behind my house, there's a creek. It's filled with dark, cold water that reflects the thick and sticky mud-soaked riverbed. There's a row of short pine trees skirting the creek's edge, stunted as if they've been hammered into the ground until just their tops showed, providing shade that only a child could enjoy. The grass squishes underfoot as you get closer to the water, gulping up each approaching footstep as if it were a thirsty animal. Canary grass and cattails entangle and untangle in a breeze that sends the quaking aspen rocking and whispering against the sky.

I'm ten years old and I come here to catch frogs. It's an after-school ritual shared by my closest friends and me. We rush home after the final dismissal bell, toss our backpacks at the bottom of the deck stairs, and sprint to the water, our laughter filling the air like wind chimes. We tiptoe along the shore, through reeds and weeds still crisp from a harsh winter. With endless practice, we've learned how to tread lightly so our steps are nearly silent. The water is still, the surface like maple taffy. We know this is a ruse. There's life bustling below; we need only wake it up. We start slow and low, sound softly rumbling in our throats. Guttural. Glottal. Let it reverberate and then let it fall. Wait a beat until we try again. The sound is both foreign and familiar, one we've taught ourselves and learned by ear. Three calls, one response. Then another, timid and quiet, and another and another, until the entire pond is filled with the chirping and croaking of wood frogs and spring peepers. My friends and I share in a thrilled glance before gleefully cheering and shouting our success into the bush that surrounds us.

This is, perhaps, my first remembered experience with the visceral and deep connection we form with land language that isn't taught but still learned. Every sound we let slip is foreign, filled with words that will remain unknown. And yet we glean some understanding, and there we take pride in a shared mysterious conversation with our amphibian counterparts.

There was something about learning to speak frog that felt natural. I never questioned my pronunciation or worried that I sounded silly. The goal was to get the frogs to come out of their hiding spots so we could watch them, not to start up deep discussions. So I made noise and spoke until what I was saying sounded close to what they were saying. It wasn't perfect, I knew that, but it felt right in my throat and on my tongue, so I let it live.

What I hadn't realized back then was that I had found a kinship in that animal language. And in some strange way, speaking confidently in what I'm sure was incorrect frog was my first step in rediscovering my own land language.

Anishnaabemowin should be my first language. It should be how I speak to my parents, aunties, and friends. I should be able to use it to talk to elders. I should be able to sing as easily as I know how to swear. But I can't.

I grew up learning to speak English and French in a school named after the north wind. We all spoke with rez accents, dropping and adding h's at leisure. Everyone on the rez spoke English, swore in French, and joked in Anishnaabemowin—or, at least, with what little they knew.

When I was around ten, my school introduced us to Algonquin. My entire class took the lessons for granted. We misbehaved almost every day. All we wanted was to survive that last hour before recess or lunch or dismissal. And why did we need to learn this, anyway? It wasn't as if there were enough people around who spoke it to make it worth our while. We didn't see the importance of learning and speaking something that, to us, was dead and gone.

There are fewer than a handful of fluent speakers of my language at home. While I may not have seen it as a child, I now know how precious they are. It is our duty to protect them and the knowledge they carry. Things are slowly getting better with the addition of regular Algonquin classes at school, but that doesn't mean reclaiming the language has become any easier.

In the end, those early lessons didn't exactly work. I learned a few phrases here and there—basics like "Can I go to the bathroom?" and "Can I get a drink of water?"—but learning Anishnaabemowin in a class setting couldn't happen. After all, it's a language that lives in the land and was meant to be learned out on it. Like learning to speak to frogs, I had to simply live the language.

I used to dance fancy at powwows when I was a little girl. I loved it, especially the spinning on the honour beats. I joined after-school groups where we were taught how to sing songs that honoured the water and the eagle and we learned to dance like crows and butterflies. Letting my culture live in my body this way was freeing. Sounding out the words to each song was like sipping honey. Hesitant, careful, and delicious. With a drum in my hand

and moccasins on my feet, I felt closer than ever to who I was as an Anishnaabekwe. I would dance at ceremony and at powwows. I sang with our little drum group and I loved it. But even then, something held me back. I began to doubt my "Nativeness" because I didn't look the part. And as I got older, I became increasingly aware of the fact that my face didn't match up with what I was told was Native. Now I know that such thinking is a direct product of the colonial mindset, one that has been force-fed to all Indigenous people for generations. A system that has been hoping to eradicate us has also been trying to define us for centuries. They tell us to stop being Indian, but also try to tell us we aren't Indian enough. It's worked so well that even at twelve years old, I felt uncomfortable in my skin and that I shouldn't speak my language or dance my culture because I wasn't enough.

I remember we had an assembly at my elementary school where I was asked to dance with some of the other Grade 7 fancy shawl girls. When it was done, a kid in Grade 2 came up to me and said, "You didn't know what you were doing, right? I could tell."

She didn't mean it to hurt me the way it did. She even said it with a smile. As if it was supposed to comfort me.

I smiled back as best I could and said, "Everyone has their own style."

It shouldn't have been the reason I stopped dancing, but I don't remember doing it after that. I had felt closer to who I was as an Indigenous woman when I danced, but if it had been so obvious to some seven-year-old kid that I knew nothing about the dance, what did I actually know?

So I stopped everything. I didn't dance. I didn't sing. I avoided ceremony and certainly didn't speak my language. The newly regained bit of my ancestors I had found through the physical language of our culture had slipped away from me. It happened slowly. Piece by piece, the shawl I had created for myself unwound.

In high school, I did what I could to blend in. We had a resource centre—more of a room tucked away at the far end of the school—where all the Native kids went to hang out every day. I rarely went. Some part of me—the part that believed that settler voice—felt like I didn't fit in. I wasn't Native enough. I clung to that belief for years, only seeing my Indigeneity as some sort of party trick or way to make myself seem more interesting than I was. After all, wasn't that what being different was all about?

University brought more of the same. I lived in residence my first year and was placed on a floor with people studying music history, theory, composition, and performance—just like me. Some were singers; others played woodwind, brass, piano, strings, and even the harp. It was fascinating. I came from a tiny music department that could barely afford the upkeep of the brass and woodwind instruments they had, let alone support something as healthy as orchestral strings. I made friends with people from all over Canada. I was thrilled to get to know them and learn their lived experiences and to share mine. One day, my new friends and I returned from a "floor meeting" where all residents of the second-floor wing had gathered in the common area. We were all music majors at a university program that prided itself as one of the best in the country, so the group was predominantly "elite" and white. A fact that, I'm sure, the school would say was a fluke and not a direct result of the best pre-university training being accessible only to those who could afford private lessons and top-quality instruments, but that's a topic for another essay.

"It's so weird, huh?" said my friend. "Other than that Métis guy, there are no people of colour here."

"What?" I replied. "I'm right here. I'm Algonquin."

She looked at me and raised her eyebrows. "Yeah, but you're pale. You're practically white."

Just like that, she erased me. I let her because I didn't know better. How was I supposed to respond to something like that? She wasn't exactly wrong. I *am* pale. At first glance, I don't look like a stereotype. I don't go around wearing buckskins or feathers and I certainly don't paint with the colours of the wind. But did that give her permission to ignore my identity? It spoke to her privilege and her ignorance and to the simple fact that she was behaving like a jishkish.

It has taken me a long time to find the confidence to live in the body and the skin I've been given. I'm constantly othered by a settler colonial society that tells me I'm both too much and not enough all at once—a Westernized mindset that tries to set the parameters and requirements of what it means to be a good and proper Native. To speak my language feels strange, performative, disingenuous. At times, I feel like even something as simple as saying meegwetch instead of "thank you" is inauthentic. Like I'm playing a part for someone else and not for myself. Who am I speaking my language for? Am I trying to prove my Indigeneity by using a few choice words in a language I embody but do not understand?

So much of how I feel about Anishnaabemowin is dependent on my body. I am uncomfortable with this strange space that I take up. I dance jingle now, but that didn't come easily. I spent a long time worrying that people would see me in regalia and think, "She doesn't even look Native—who does she think she is?" As if my pale skin, a constant reminder of colonialism and what it has done to change the face of Indigeneity in this country, would make me less than someone who was darker. I was afraid of the culture cops, Natives who would point and jeer and tell me I couldn't ever hope to be as culturally pure as they were. I know now that this behaviour wasn't their fault, but rather something they were taught as a by-product of colonialism. Still, I spent much of my life feeling tainted and that I had no right to speak Anishnaabemowin. I've worked hard (am still working hard) to unlearn that way of thinking. Decolonizing my body takes time, but I will get there.

Holding on to the words of my ancestors is like trying to catch river water. It is slippery, rushing, powerful, intangible. Language shapeshifts, and it asks me to do the same. Until I can find a way to accept that my Indigeneity is not defined by someone else's image, I will continue to speak my language quietly. But that small act holds power. Each word, phrase, joke, and syllable is like a prayer, like medicine.

My language is my act of self-love. Letting it breathe and expand into being feels right, even if, at times, I feel afraid. And though it may not be correct, my Anishnaabemowin is present and alive and healing. My body will remember this language that it was never truly taught, but still it learns. And speaking it will be like awakening an entire pond full of frogs who are eager to sing their replies.

Onadotân. Nîmi. Nigamo.

Melissa Bull

ENGLISH BABY

I am caught between two worlds, neither of which is fully mine, both of which are partially mine.

—ADA MARÍA ISASI-DÍAZ

Je suis deux. I lead two lives. Doubled, *dubbée.* My jaw clicks up and down but my words slide out sideways.

I've been told my voice and demeanour change entirely when I switch from French to English. I'm not filtering my English personality into my French voice or vice versa; I'm not a tourist in either, I'm different in each. Words shape how you think. Cultural norms impact the way that words are expressed. But the thresholds of any culture, of either of my cultures, are porous and each of my personalities leaks into the other. I am an excitable anglo, speaking in uncomfortable decibels. Those same florid intonations may read emotionless and deadpan in French. Though I regularly make Gallic syntactic slips in my spoken English (rarely in writing), my English is looser—I speak it with peers and bosses, friends, teachers, colleagues.

I've studied more English than French literature. I write almost exclusively in English. My French is more contained, spoken mostly with my mother (who, as she had me later in life, is two generations removed from me) and with my partner, his child, my half-siblings, some friends and acquaintances. When I'm tired, I slip back into English for precision. My partner understands and answers in French, which is what I prefer. Most intra-linguistic couples fall into a habit of speaking the winner's English. I don't want us to do that. I want the push, the opportunity, the space to become ever more fluent in my withered maternal tongue.

WHO WOULD I BE had my family sent me to French school?

Would I be as I think I am but am not exactly (when your identity is hybrid, you may learn to define yourself by how others define you, which is by exclusion, like a multiple-choice question when you're not sure of the answer), a francophone civilian and an English-language writer? Or would I have been a French-language writer who occasionally read in English?

What would my English accent sound like? Halting, crashes of ill-selected slang with a twist American twang I'd have lifted from TV? Would I have aspirated or added the letter *h* at incongruous moments, confusing *airs* with *hairs*.

Would my French family, cousins, siblings, aunts, and uncles still call me *l'anglaise* if my French was familiarly accented of home, rather than with the bland, unrooted, no-place banality I talk through now? (Are you Belgian? people ask, searching to place my accent.)

Who would I have been if I'd been raised in my mother tongue? If I'd been raised to speak the same language as my four older half-siblings, Pascale, Alain, Samia, Bruno. All of whom speak little English. (Caesura.)

What would I have written. *Autofiction, récits, histoires, nouvelles?*

What would my morals have been? Would I still have strived for some internalized example of upper-class Protestantism because of how exotic it seemed, how orderly, how proper. We do the right thing the right thing they hum and hum and hum. So good so right so good so right. Would the promise of Protestant virtue have wormed its way into me had I been raised in my own mother's tongue and in the context of home?

What vocabulary flares would I throw out for fun? With full mastery of the mother tongue I do not now master or come close to mastering. (You couldn't tell, you'd compliment me on my non-accent and admit to preferring French from France. Imagine saying that about the Canadian accent: I can't understand a word you're saying, I only listen to the BBC.)

Who would Mélissa have been? How has Melissa never measured up to her? How much of that is my own fault? Lack of cultural follow-through. Cowardice in the face of divisive politics. Tears at any show of patriotism. (On the one hand vs. on the other—the constant sidling of a hybrid self, never trusting claims of a hermetic identity, of a definitive take on history.)

How much did my mother's previous marriage to a Lebanese man and her relationship with my stepfather, James, who was younger than her and Black, a manager at McDonald's, play into my WASP father getting custody of me when my parents divorced? (WASP culture a melisma of right and good and proper, the myopic impossibility of recognizing other cultures as valid, valuable, worthy.)

Whatever the cause, my father, Rob, got custody and applied for special dispensation to send me to English school. I grew up borrowing the English accents of my classmates and envying them and their families (I measure love; I envy love), taking on their English-accented French and coming home with marbles in my mouth, no longer able to express myself with the blithe and easy comfort of my own cadences. And I grew up and became an English-language writer. Because my English father was an English writer with a basement full of English books and a booming English radio voice I'd stay up past my bedtime to hear on the clock radio in the hall.

MY MOTHER, SUZANNE, is dying. Her doctor—whose name is Stern, and she reminds me of a tern, with her tidy chestnut hair and small stature—has told us my mother has until mid-July to live. *"J'ai marqué ma date d'expiration dans mon calendrier,"* my mother said. *"Le 15 juillet."* This date has since passed. She's stopped wearing her wig. She takes morphine and steroids *en alternance*.

My mother was born in an apartment over a general store in Rivière-du-Loup in 1938 to Conrad, a travelling salesman (he kept a bronze medallion of St. Christopher in his pocket) and his wife, Laurette, a former bank teller and the family beauty. My mother was born on the cusp of La Grande Noirceur, two years before women were granted the right to vote in Quebec. She is eighty-two years old and lives alone in her tiny, nineteenth-century home in the working-class borough of Saint-Henri, in Montreal. To call it a house would be generous. It is something between a cottage and a shack. A witch's hut. My mother's an installation artist and her house is cluttered to its sloping eaves with objects she has collected for potential projects or just because they delighted her: taxidermied birds of prey, bolts of lace, multi-storeyed dollhouses, insect statuettes. She lives alone because the pandemic has made hospitals dangerous. But she's lived alone since her last—her third—divorce, almost thirty years ago, because it suits her. She doesn't like to be around people. Across the street from her house, train yards. Her crooked blue-green gabled cottage, built at the time when a river ran down from Westmount to Saint-Henri (I recall its name as Rivière à la Loutre—Otter River—but I could be wrong), when men tanned cattle hides and rinsed them in that river—shudders with every passing train.

My mother's last name is Blouin. Her mother's maiden name, printed clearly on each of her hospital bracelets, was Tardif. Our Blouin ancestors, originally from the Loire Valley or La Rochelle, arrived in Quebec sometime in the 1660s. The Tardifs are descended from Olivier Letardif, born in Brittany in 1601, who sailed to Quebec with Samuel de Champlain in 1621. Letardif was a translator of Indigenous languages. I imagine unknown swindlings and tragedies associated with his skill. His life's work an open port to the European settler's project of white supremacy; a project built for his kin, for me to benefit from directly, in a line I can trace right to him (and to others arrived from Brittany by tall-masted ships). I acknowledge that. I hold that. (In the one hand.) I also imagine his intelligence and curiosity, a powerful desire to understand other ways of life. (In the other.) He managed Canada's (La Nouvelle-France's) first trading company, la Compagnie des Cents Associés. His wife, Barbe Émard, was thirteen when they married. A jangling pocket of facts I can barely imagine.

My father's family—Bulls, Hendersons, Shores, mostly Irish Protestant—settled in and around Brampton, Ontario, in the 1820s. They were blacksmiths, tuba players, innkeepers, sheriffs (the bad kind, the Irish cop kind, I think), organ players, one-room-schoolhouse teachers. They strapped their kids for playing old maid on Sundays, sang in harmony, forked over their house down payments in cash. (The right thing the right thing the right thing.)

VERY FEW ENGLISH-SPEAKING Canadians immigrate to Quebec. Most English-speaking Canadians who live in Quebec lead a parallel existence, both feet firmly planted in Canada, cheap digs in Montreal. Many have learned some French. In school, because of Trudeau Sr. Which is nice, of course. Thank you. Genuinely. For going to that trouble. I don't mean that sarcastically. I'm amazed and grateful. But they can't really understand Québécois French, have learned to denigrate the French accent here, never considering that—much like the differences between British English(es) and North American English(es)—European French and North American French are different. That there are historical reasons for this. That this difference is not a diminishment. We are speaking real, legitimate French. As French as Canadian English is English.

Canadian residents in Quebec do not often attend any of the fifty-ish French-language theatres between Montreal and Quebec City, though the plays often tour around the world, are celebrated in Europe, may be translated into English, German, Catalan. They do not watch even Oscar-nominated French films made in Quebec, read internationally recognized French-language literature, watch French-language TV, or listen to French podcasts. They live cheaply here in Montreal, often in a neighbourhood called Mile End. It's like expat Canadian Portland. But they don't know they live in New York City. English-speakers from the ROC who live in Montreal often tell me they don't want to travel to other neighbourhoods or attend French-language events because they worry about speaking French improperly and being judged (and they worry it will be bad). Perhaps because they learned French as a thing of grammar, they are concerned they will be quizzed, as if Quebec were a test and not a thriving, multi-dimensional culture, collection of cultures. They don't realize how often they are asking French people, whose English may not be as strong as their French, to do all the work. They are not excited about a culture unique in all of the Americas. They don't wonder how this perspective might be different to their own (different revolutions, different insights). They wish we'd just get over it. They joke about Céline Dion and roll their eyes, pretending a knowingness they haven't earned.

MY FATHER MOVED to Montreal to cover the Quiet Revolution for the *Montreal Star*, a now-defunct newspaper. They didn't have any bilingual reporters on staff. They asked him did he speak French, he stammered, *"Oui!"* and he was hired on the spot.

He met my mother one night at Sir Winston Churchill Pub on Crescent Street. She was crying at the bar—she missed her bearded Scottish boyfriend who could have been my father's doppelgänger—and my bearded father scooped her up. *"Je pense qu'il s'est assis dans la même chaise,"* she told me. They married in a Protestant church in Toronto in 1974. My anglophone grandmother, Hilda, asked my mother, "Do they still speak French in Quebec?" And was surprised to hear that indeed they did. She was not initially enthused about a francophone Catholic divorcée with four adolescent Lebanese children marrying her son. Likewise, my French grandmother almost didn't attend the wedding, as she was concerned about burning in Hell for setting foot in a Protestant church (schisms upon schisms). I was born a few years later and baptized Catholic in Saint-Denys church in Sainte-Foy. On the birth certificate my name reads Mélissa Élizabeth Bull. I've been told it looks pretentious to spell it with the accent in English, so I dropped it. But when I first learned to write my name, it was in all caps: MÉLISSA BULL. My father liked to tell the story of how, as a toddler, I pointed to myself and said, *"Mélissa Élizabeth... mais où est la bulle?"* (There are two ways to say my last name in French. Either you say *"bulle,"* meaning "bubble," or you say *"boules,"* "balls"—which does not mean "testicles" in French, but "tits." Which means that unless you're very careful to pronounce my name the English way, my name in French is Mélissa Tits.)

I grew up for a time, while my parents were still together, with two of my adolescent half-sisters, Pascale and Samia, who were seventeen and fourteen when I was born, and they and my mother spoke and sang, rocked and tucked and bathed and fed me, in French. Though my father spoke to me in English, I called him *Papa*, naturally, since we spoke French at home. Later, if English people overheard me speaking to my father, they told me how affected that sounded.

But of course you call your parent by the word for parent in your language. (Hybrid identities are held in tight check. Your culture is showing, tuck it in.)

"YOU WERE NEW life being born into an old world," my father always told me on my birthday.

"I wanted to have an English baby," my mother once told me. She also said, "Your father had kind eyes, so I wanted to give him a baby." And: "One time when I was pregnant with you, I drank some beer and climbed into a police sidecar. Everyone was laughing!" (She said this in French.)

I had two French teachers from Quebec in all of my schooling—my kindergarten teacher, Michelle-Marie, and my fifth-grade teacher, Linda. English kids at school called me a "French pepper." Canadians think you get called a frog when you're francophone, but that's derision for the French from Francers, not Quebecers. We get called peppers because of a class thing—the Pepsi company in Montreal's east end notoriously hired a lot of francophones, once upon a time, though no one remembered that story by the time they attributed the moniker to me. I soon dropped my native accent and began speaking French poorly to fit in better. My French family, of course, noticed I'd flipped sides. My middle half-sister, Samia, told my mother it was a mistake to send me to English school. She was worried about my growing up in a separate culture from the rest of my family. It's a good question: why did my parents pur-posely choose to raise me in a different culture from my siblings? Still today, this intentional rift is a mystery. Maybe my father simply chose to raise me in his own culture and didn't overthink it. (What class issues may have been at work within him to drive this choice?) Whatever the reason, his decision isolated me from my family. There are great riches in a hybrid culture. Valuable lessons about identity when you are neither/nor. When you feel the stitches that suture one part of you to another. But it is also a kind of loss. (You hold the richness and the loss with both hands.)

My brilliant mother, who had grown up in La Grande Noirceur, in a time when women were explicitly discouraged from any post-secondary education, when dancing and shorts were forbidden, when priests checked in to ensure women were performing their wifely duties (what I mean is: priests visited my mother to hassle her to have sex with her husband), when great swaths of literature were noted in a list of banned books called L'Index, and contraception was illegal, my mother, whose four francophone children were taken away from her in her first custody battle, had reinvented herself as a person who lived in English, a world she viewed as more open. Today she counters that she is as bicultural as I am. (Shortly after I published a collection of poetry, she began to write in English herself—and even plagiarized one of my poems and won a prize.) Switching teams, living in English, allowed her to present herself anew. Though she worked exclusively in French and we speak French with one another, after meeting my father, her reading, her television, and her love affairs were all conducted in English. My mother emigrated from Quebec to Canada, all the while remaining in Montreal.

ENGLISH LITERARY CULTURE in Montreal hurts my stomach a little. Anglophones typically plan English-only events. If I suggest inviting francophone authors, they tell me now isn't the time for inclusion with French. I have, on occasion, received emails from people saying they once took French in high school, can I please recommend the top three award-winning poetry books they should translate because they know they could do it if someone would only tell them what was good. You don't have to be fluent to translate, they explain. (But do you know the sound of this choice? The Cours Classique accent in that one? The intertextual reference? The decision for archaic words here? The echoes of our winters? Virtue-signalling as substitution for conversations, for encounters, for the work.)

MY ENGLISH FAMILY doesn't consider me Québécoise. ("Those people just want to break up my country.") I pass as anglo and, as my culture is not meaningful to them, it simply doesn't register. (How often does the dominant white culture do this to people? Much more than I see. How much do I participate in this erasure unknowingly myself?) My French family thinks of me as English. (My identity attached to the RCMP, the redcoats, the Queen of England, the oppressors, the English minority authorities remarking snidely to the Franco majority they rule over that they don't speak French. The English as storm troopers.)

These perceptions will not change. (History is a living thing.)

Those of us who carry more than one identity are an amalgamation of what our families and peers have told us we are. As much as what they have told us we are not, when they stand as gatekeepers of their own hermetic cultures. (When you are two, you are never enough of one or the other.) For homogenous communities, cultural choices aren't seen as choices but rather as eventualities. Being more than one culture provokes constant tension around the notion of choice, of expression. Identification versus identity. Any sense of home is a fraught negotiation. There will be no resolution.

While my name is Mélissa and while my mother tongue is French, you can hear my English education in my accent. I make typos in French (they're called shells, *des coquilles*, in French). I could never work as a French-language editor. I will never really write in French; in French, I'm always playing catch-up. There are huge gaps in my knowledge of Quebec culture. Important people I haven't read, music I don't know. My French is broken.

MY MOTHER WEARS her father's St. Christopher medal on a chain around her neck. It used to dangle from the rear-view mirror of her 1978 Westfalia. She holds the bronze disk in her hand. Her strong and nimble artist hands are the only parts of her body that haven't wasted away. She shows me where the engraving of the saint has almost disappeared. *"Pour mon dernier voyage,"* she says.

I'M TOO OLD to have children; I never had any, and now I won't. But I can name myself, even now, so late in life. I recently applied to double-barrel my patronym, to add my mother's to my father's: Mélissa Blouin-Bull. Marrying both cultures (identification as identity), creating an uncomfortable, unpronounceable mouthful. *Un trait d'union.*

Leonarda Carranza

LENGUA MATERNA

When I was seven I fell hard for English. It was a messy toxic love born out of racial injury, self-doubt, and insecurity. English did not love me back.

We came to Canada as refugees from El Salvador. I entered a Toronto classroom without knowing a single word of English. I didn't know how to ask for help or how to say the word *washroom*. I remember a group of kids huddled together and laughing at me, a girl's toothy smile. They were asking me to pronounce the word *three*. Instead, I kept saying *tree*, and they kept asking and laughing, and no matter how hard I tried I couldn't get my mouth to make the sound they wanted. They laughed and laughed so hard. I felt like I was being pushed down and made to feel less for something I couldn't control. Learning English came with these feelings of ridicule and shame. These experiences tamed me, made me want to give up parts of myself, and shamed me into hating my tongue and the accent it made.

It took me many years to realize what was happening. This wasn't love.

AFTER A YEAR in Canada, I started to feel comfortable in English. I remember one day wanting to hear my new sound. I used an old cassette player to record myself. I don't remember what I said on the recording. I just remember the feeling of hot shame rising to my face when I heard the thickness of my Spanish tongue.

I deleted the recording.

DAD THOUGHT SPANISH belonged to us or that we belonged to it. He wanted us to feel proud and to fight to preserve our language. He didn't hate English. Back in El Salvador, he had studied English in high school, and when he came to Canada, he was able to speak and feel understood. Maybe he wanted us to learn English without falling in love with it. Or maybe, when he saw the way we salivated over American movies, music, and fashion, how we started reading and writing exclusively in English, maybe he resented how quickly our alliances drifted farther away from him.

English was harder for Mom, who had chosen to study German in high school and who, unlike most of her classmates, never dreamt of migrating to the us nor imagined living in Canada. When we first arrived, she took English classes out of necessity. Not out of some aspiration to one day read English literature or watch Canadian films, not out of any interest in possessing English or being possessed by it, and not because she was falling in love with a new country. English was a means to access work, and she was lucky her first English teacher was kind and treated her like a friend. But, like most working-poor racialized women, Mom's time for schooling in those early years was cut short. We needed money and it wasn't long before she was forced to start working. She was offered a job that required very little competency and where she worked for eight hours a day on an assembly line making antennas.

It would be more than a decade before she would take another English class.

WHEN I WAS A TEEN, Spanish was something boys found sexy about me. *Say something in Spanish,* they would say. I wonder how these boys might have felt about me if I'd spoken words in the hushing sounds of the Nahuatl language? Would they still ask me to pronounce words in my language?

ONE SUMMER WHEN I was in my thirties, Mom told me for the first time how insecure she still feels in English. Even after so many years of living in Canada, she still feels like English does not belong to her. She told me how she always wanted at least one of us to partner with someone who spoke Spanish.

"You don't know how hard it is," she told me in Spanish while we sat in her backyard. I wore sunglasses and Mom stared right at me. The heaviness of needing to feel understood and at ease in language imprinted itself into the memory of that day.

None of us did find Spanish-speaking partners and, sadly, this isn't the only way Mom feels left out or excluded. At family gatherings, my siblings and I may start off talking about a movie we recently watched or a book we read or even share something from the news and the conversation will inevitably drift into English. It takes us a while to register that Mom isn't participating. Sometimes she interrupts us and asks us to explain something; sometimes she leaves the room without us noticing.

One day, she called to ask me how to tell the plumber that the pipe was leaking. It reminded me how much she still needs us to find the right words. As a child, my mother often relied on me to translate. I hated the responsibility. I hated the proximity to adults and their conversations. All I wanted was for Mom to hurry up and learn so she could do it herself. I didn't realize that Mom was forced to work. And the work that was available to her perpetuated a lack of access to the time, energy, and money necessary to learn a new language.

Try working an eight-hour shift in a factory, travelling more than two hours each way, and then coming home to make dinner and then grocery shop on weekends and do laundry and clean a house, and see where you can fit language learning into your day. Mom spent her time isolated while the rest of us went to school, made friends, and started to plant roots in this country. While we were busy learning a new language, she was left behind.

WHEN WE WERE children, my siblings and I were not allowed to speak English at home. This forced us to keep speaking Spanish, although we often ran upstairs and into our rooms to speak secretly in English with each other. I always thought this was my father's rule. I thought he was so committed to preserving our Latinx identity and our connection to the Spanish language that he insisted we speak only Spanish in the house. It's only recently that I learned that it was Mom who created this rule to help us all preserve the language.

FOR THE FIRST FEW years in Canada, we thought we were only going to stay until the war ended. We couldn't have known that the war would take twelve years and that when it was finally over we'd feel like there was no place to go back to. Mom lost two brothers in the war. One brother was taken by the military and tortured. Her youngest was killed and left on the side of the road. Her father and sister died while we were living in Canada, and the home we had in El Salvador was taken from us, stolen by a relative who took advantage of our situation. Almost everyone she loved was taken from her.

For Mom, learning English came with the necessity and urgency to find work to feed and house our family. It also came with the guilt of leaving family and community behind and then the grief of losing them. It came with feeling left out and being pushed down and ridiculed.

When she finally decided to return to school in her mid-forties, more than a decade after we first arrived, she was filled with self-doubt. Hadn't it been too long already? Wasn't she too old now to learn the language? In class, the instructor asked her to introduce herself. He asked how many children she had, and when she told him she had six, he looked at her with disgust.

"Is that how you spent your life?" he demanded to know in front of everyone. He made her feel small, like she didn't belong in that classroom.

FOR A WHILE in my twenties, I stopped speaking to Mom exclusively in Spanish and started to sprinkle our conversation first with English words and then with complete English phrases. I stopped from a place of carelessness. And then I justified my choice. If I lost fluency or stayed at a childlike level, well, what was the harm?

During that time, I started to learn more about the brutality of colonization in Central America and the role the Spanish language played in the violence inflicted on the Pipil, Maya Chortí, Maya Pocomam, Cacaopera, and Lenca people. I felt contempt toward my mother tongue and the role it played in erasing our ancestral languages. I didn't feel belonging in Spanish. And I couldn't muster any pride in a language that was part of a strategy to eradicate us. It wasn't as if I was valorizing English over Spanish. I knew the violent colonial role that English played and plays throughout the world. English was just convenient. Wasn't I merely swapping one colonial tongue for another?

I couldn't see that Mom never had that choice. Spanish was bound to her in ways I couldn't understand.

AS YOUNG KIDS, we took aim at Mom's lack of fluency. We had been taught that our accent was something that should be made fun of. And we were good students. We laughed when she mispronounced words. We made her feel ashamed and fearful of making mistakes. How can anyone learn a language under those circumstances?

As children, we couldn't understand how hard it must've been for her to have to start over in a new country with the responsibility of supporting her whole family. Today, I tell her it was because of all the violence and shaming that English was hard and still is hard for her. She nods quietly when I say this.

This isn't just her story. There is so much violence and humiliation and shaming tied to learning English for working-poor racialized women. So much was thrown onto her body and, of course, the body still carries that.

Even today, I see the way people treat her, the way they get tired of listening to her when she's asking for something. A few months ago, we drove to Ottawa and stopped in a small town to order bagels and coffee. When I came out of the washroom, she was asking the white cashier for a bagel, and just in the short time I was beside her, she must've repeated herself over five times. The cashier still could not understand her. I had to shout the word *bagel* at her. And I thought, why the fuck is it so hard to understand an accent?

"HOW OLD WERE YOU when you came to Canada?" people often ask.

They know that languages are swallowed up in this place. Despite never attending any formal schooling in El Salvador, I am completely fluent. I didn't think of my mother's work in passing on the language until I saw how surprised folks are when they realize I still speak Spanish. We know so many Latinx families that opted to speak only English at home so they could strip their tongues of their accents. My younger siblings came to Canada under the age of five. They are fluent speakers and readers. Like me, they only learned the language from speaking at home, mostly with our mother. My youngest brother was born in Toronto, and when he went to school his first year, his only language was Spanish.

Mom's first English teacher and friend was the one who warned her not to talk to us in English. "You'll suffer," she had said. "Because it will be harder for you to pick up the language without their help, but they will keep their mother tongue and that is far more important."

SEVENTEEN YEARS AGO, when my sister had her first child, she chose not to teach her Spanish. Back then it didn't seem like a big deal. By then I had grown disillusioned with the Spanish language. Wouldn't it be more meaningful if we all learned Nahuatl? If we reclaimed our ancestral tongue? But over time, this choice not to pass on the language to her first child or the next child began to feel significant. I noticed how we used my niece's and nephew's inabilities for our benefit, sometimes choosing to speak Spanish to keep them from knowing things. There were times when they felt far away from us, like when they were left out of all our Spanish jokes. Times when they missed out on the people my siblings and I become when we speak our mother tongue. We couldn't watch Spanish movies or shows with them. We couldn't share the music we love. But mostly, I noticed how they missed out on fully knowing their grandma. Mom speaks to them in English but sometimes asks for help to translate some of the words. They see the part of her that stumbles in language. They don't get to know her sharp tongue, the way she plays with language—makes up new words—the way her humour comes alive in Spanish.

And seeing the distance between my sister's children and Mom, I reconsidered the value of Spanish.

ONE YEAR, I GOT a job in Nicaragua and then after the contract was over I travelled through Central America. I realized what a gift it was to be able to communicate, to feel heard, and to feel fully understood. I started to read in Spanish and found stories I felt were speaking directly to me. And then one summer I went back to El Salvador with

Mom and I got to see the village where she grew up. I met her cousins and my cousins for the first time. We talked and laughed with each other, and I got to experience Mom at home with community speaking her language. Spanish was more than a colonial tongue. It was also packed tight with our culture and beliefs. Spanish was the door and the bridge to Central America, the culture, the land, the people. And throughout the trip, I experienced something that Canada had always withheld from me. I felt moments of belonging.

WHEN THE PANDEMIC BREAKS, Mom and I are stripped bare of all our routines. For weeks, I worry if she's safe and eating enough. And finally, she comes and stays with me. And the days are unending and time breaks and we lose parts of ourselves. I can't go into work and Mom can't see her friends. Together we distract ourselves with the rise and fall of daily COVID cases in our city. And our city, populated by racialized working-poor communities, goes into lockdown after lockdown. Spanish colours our days and pushes against the greys of panic. Spanish flows out of me with ease and breathes aliveness into the stuckness. And even though I'm anxious and there is a pandemic raging outside, inside Mom is making pan dulce and we're craving tamales and plátanos fritos and dreaming of all the gatherings we will have when this is over. And it feels like my childhood again, when Mom was the centre of my world. And I think about the language between us and if this closeness could even be possible without Spanish.

I ask Mom if she ever worried when we first came to Canada and she saw us turning rapidly toward English.

She looks straight at me. She doesn't hesitate. "Yes," she says. "I thought a day would come when we wouldn't understand each other."

And I think what a fool I would have been if I'd lost my mother tongue. In my act of rebellion, I would have lost all the words, all the language, that leads back to my mother.

Adam Pottle

NEWBORN

wasn't supposed to be there.

My play *The Black Drum* had just finished its initial run at Soul-pepper Theatre in Toronto. It ran to the end of June 2019. Opening night was a revelation: the performers, directors, choreographers, and designers had taken my measly blueprint of a script and transformed it into a spectacular fever dream of a play. The colours popped off the stage; the performers' Signed Music left beautiful dents in the audiences' memories. It was the world's first-ever all-Deaf musical, and the reviews were raves.

A week after closing night, all of us—cast and crew—sat near the gate at Toronto Pearson Airport awaiting our flight to Paris. From there, cars would take us to Reims, France, the site of Festival Clin d'Oeil, the world's largest international Deaf arts festival. Every two years, thousands of Deaf people descend on Reims to experience plays, films, and musical acts, all of them performed in Sign Languages from around the world.

I wasn't supposed to be there.

WHEN WE LANDED in Paris, we—all ten cast members, our producers, designers, stage managers, choreographers, publicists, and myself—loaded into the cars for the hour-long trip to Reims. We all sat in the back, the seats facing each other. I rode with one of our cast members and our set and prop designer. The cast member, an experienced actor with several theatre and TV credits, including Broadway, signs beautifully. Even simple phrases take on a unique poetry, like watching milk flow from a waterfall.

Yet I found it difficult to understand him. Although I was born Deaf, I grew up in a hearing family and was expected to conform to the world of sound. I never learned Sign Language growing up. When I was eight, I took one class in Signed English. The lessons quickly faded. It's difficult to maintain a language when there's no one to converse with. In school I wore hearing aids and FM systems. The accommodations set me apart; I always felt self-conscious. I chafed against the hearing world.

I began learning American Sign Language in 2014, when I was thirty. Learning a language is like finding individual stitches in a pattern; fluency is being able to take those stitches and weave them into a tapestry, which is exactly what the cast members of *The Black Drum* do. I, on the other hand, was still trying to recognize the stitches that formed that beautiful tapestry, and in the car I felt a familiar discomfort: the barbed push-and-pull of being ensnared between the Deaf and hearing worlds. I tried to understand the actor and the designer—the former Deaf, the latter hearing—but soon discomfort gave way to anxiety, and I withdrew from conversation and stared out the window at France's vast green fields. ·

THE BLACK DRUM tells the story of Joan, a Deaf woman whose wife died a year prior. Joan's grief continues to dominate her, and she is soon pulled into a bizarre dream world where the landscape is monochrome and the people wear nothing but black and white. A towering authoritarian figure called the Minister rules over this world. He takes Joan's wife prisoner, and to free her, herself, and the other inhabitants of the world, Joan must battle through her grief and express the inner music she has been long repressing. She receives help from her tattoos, which come to life, and from a group of young people who, like the other inhabitants of this world, are oppressed by the Minister.

Writing the play was difficult. English does not translate directly into American Sign Language. Sign Language grammar is closer to Japanese than to English. To ask, "What is your name?" in ASL, one says, "Name you," while lowering one's eyebrows. Facial expressions are as much a part of grammar as the signs themselves, and I had to keep this in mind while writing.

I wrote several different drafts. All of them were scrapped. They were too verbose, the characters' motives unclear. There was either too much material for the actors or not enough. I had to write according to how words look and feel onstage, not how they sound. To write the story properly, I had to let go of and rebel against my upbringing and my reading experience, all of which was based on hearing notions of writing. All my previous poetry and fiction had focused chiefly on hearing characters and on a hearing perception of language. All the poets and novelists and dramatists I'd read had to be scraped from my mind.

In December 2018, six months before the play's premiere, I travelled to Oslo, Norway, to work with the director, Mira Zuckermann, who runs Teater Manu, a Deaf theatre company. Oslo is a gorgeous city, especially in the winter, when one can ice-skate in full view of pizza joints, Rolex stores, and luxury clothing shops.

One night I walked to the winter carnival to find something to eat. The carnival had a Ferris wheel lit up with pink and purple lights against the black sky, along with more than a dozen food vendors serving doughnuts, barbecued sausages, ice cream, and candied fruit. As I walked back toward my hotel with a sausage biscuit and

Caesar salad, a crowd of at least three hundred people holding torches came marching down the cobblestone lane toward me. The torchbearers smiled and ambled past me, gathering in the square outside the Grand Hotel, steps away from the winter carnival. Up on the hotel balcony, Nadia Murad and Dr. Denis Mukwege, that year's winners of the Nobel Peace Prize, waved to the crowd. The torchbearers in the small square held up their flames in tribute to the inner fire Murad and Mukwege had stoked in them—the fire of fellow feeling and hope for a better future.

Working in Oslo was challenging: Mira's first language is Norwegian Sign Language. But with the help of Mira's sister, Solvi, who served as an interpreter, I ended up rewriting the entire play from scratch in five days. I seldom slept, but I ended up with a draft that Mira and I were happy with. And, with a few added tweaks, that became the rehearsal script.

In theatre, the script is God. Playwrights usually have the final say in what goes onstage. With *The Black Drum*, I provided a blueprint for the actors, who, with Mira's help and the help of the choreographers and Sign Language masters, composed their own Signed Music based on the descriptions I gave in the script.

Signed Music is a fairly new concept, to the point where our production had to create a new sign to describe it. It is visual music created through the body's movements. The body does not conform to an outside rhythm; it creates the rhythm. One conjures images and emotions and whole worlds using only the body. The words in the script were never wholly mine. I trusted Mira to interpret my vision of the story and guide the actors through it.

On opening night in Toronto, I had no idea what to expect. I hadn't seen a rehearsal and had no idea what the compositions would look like. The buzz surrounding the show was positive—I'd done an interview with the CBC hours before the show—but buzz means nothing if the creators themselves aren't satisfied.

The show was a revelation. The scene designs and video projects captivated the audience. The actors' talent pulsed off the stage. It was humbling and exhilarating, and I realized the beauty that comes from communal trust in the name of creation.

I WASN'T INVITED to Reims.

Nobody had asked me if I wanted to go. I had to ask the producers if I could accompany the team. I booked my own ticket to France and applied for my own travel funding. When we arrived in Reims, I didn't receive a festival pass, which meant I couldn't join the cast and crew for meals or performances or the evening celebrations. My anxieties had become externalized: it was as though the producers thought of me as separate from the cast and crew, as though I was not Deaf enough to join them.

I never slept in Reims. Not only was it a scorching hot summer, with the temperature rising to thirty-four degrees Celsius in the daytime, but Canada was the festival's featured country, and *The Black Drum* was the featured piece. My anxiety and depression, which I'd been living with since I was ten years old, had become exacerbated.

A few months prior, in April, I'd come close to ending my life. I'd stood over the kitchen sink holding a butcher knife to my throat and began sawing through my skin. I stopped before I reached the carotid artery; my pulse thrummed against the steel blade.

A week later I began taking medication and seeing a therapist.

On our second day in Reims, I did receive a festival pass, but by then it felt like the wedge between me and my peers was permanent. The communication barrier felt insurmountable. Our cast and crew were beautiful, talented, empathetic people, but I didn't feel I belonged with them. It broke my heart.

That night, when I arrived back at the hotel, I bought a can of Coke and took it to my room. I emptied the can into the sink and crumpled and twisted it back and forth until it tore apart, leaving sharp edges in the aluminum. Using those sharp edges, I sliced myself on my left leg, cutting myself in different directions. The blood was a relief, like steam escaping a boiling pot.

For a few seconds I saw myself in the mirror. My pupils had dilated, like those of a predator. All my self-hatred, all my internalized ableism, coiled in my eyes.

After I cleaned the cuts, I went downstairs and bought a menstrual pad from the bathroom. I tore the handle off a complimentary tote bag and wrapped it around my leg, fixing the pad in place. I lay in bed for a few hours and, at 5:30 a.m., saw the sunlight seeping through the window and got up and wandered the streets. They were empty. The dawn light was spongy and welcoming.

At the far end of the street stood the Notre-Dame de Reims. The dawn light rose up behind it, framing it with a golden halo of sanctity the original architects no doubt envisioned. I walked seven blocks down the middle of the street and sat down in front of the cathedral. I glanced around. I was completely alone with this eight-hundred-year-old edifice. There was no one to talk to. There was no one to misunderstand. I didn't have to say anything. The cathedral's beauty spoke for itself.

ON THE THIRD NIGHT, I accompanied the cast and crew to the Village, where everyone could eat and drink and dance on the customized dance floor and rap along with the Deaf MCs who performed onstage. Stage lights whirled and blazed. Bass beats pounded through the ground. The arcade featured old Street Fighter and Pac-Man games. The line for the mechanical bull was long. Deaf people know how to party.

Thousands of people from all over the world had packed into the Village. Their hands fluttered in dozens of different Sign Languages, forming a chorus whose poetry and vivacity left me breathless. For the first time, I felt at home. I felt entirely comfortable with, and even grateful for, my deafness. The view was panoramic, sublime. It overwhelmed me.

My peers encouraged me to eat and talk and dance with them. People asked to take pictures with the actors, who graciously obliged. I met many wonderful people from France, America, Finland, Britain, Sweden, China, and Brazil.

Yet I remained anxious. Many of the conversations were inaccessible to me. I had so much to learn and unlearn if I wanted to be part of this world. And I wanted to. More than anything.

HUNDREDS OF PEOPLE packed into the beautiful La Comédie performance theatre for the three stagings of *The Black Drum*. The actors were spectacular, earning standing ovations after each performance.

I cried during each staging. I didn't want to. It felt self-indulgent, as though I was in awe of my own work. I wasn't. I thought I'd spent my tears back in June, or even that night back in April. I couldn't figure out why I had such a visceral reaction to what was happening onstage.

After the third performance, I asked to speak to the company. Ten minutes before speaking, I gathered my thoughts, writing them down on a piece of scrap paper. I took one of the interpreters aside and showed her what I wrote.

"I'm going to cry," she said.

"That's okay. Me too."

The cast and crew and the parents of the young performers gathered in the rehearsal studio on the second floor. Everyone was sweaty and relieved; they congratulated each other on their performance.

Our assistant director called for everyone's attention, and I stood before them. As soon as I began speaking, I had to fend off tears.

"Thank you all for your brilliant work putting this play together. I wanted to take a moment and tell you exactly what this play means to me." I sniffled. I stared at my page. If I looked at the company, I'd break down. "Every time I watch you all, and see your performances and designs, I cry. I bawl. There's a reason for that. Part of it is your great performances. Part of it is your beautiful designs and tireless efforts to keep the show going. But another part of it is the secret meaning this play has for me.

"This play is about oppression, love, freedom, friendship, grief . . . but it's also about mental illness."

My voice cracked. "I am mentally ill. I have depression and anxiety. It's something I've struggled with this year. And on this trip. It blots the happiness out of my world, and I can't see it. I can't enjoy life, no matter how beautiful it is."

The sobs began building. I pressed on.

"But when I see you all perform, when I see your grace, intelligence, beauty, talent, and love on full display, it gives me hope, and that overwhelms me. Thank you all for giving me hope—for showing me light and colour amidst the darkness."

I broke. I covered my face with my speech and began sobbing. All my exhaustion and anxiety and fear and despair from sleepless nights and a lifetime of self-doubt and self-hatred exploded out of me.

Multiple footsteps scraped on the floor and I immediately found myself in the centre of the most beautiful warmth I'd ever experienced. The entire cast and crew had run up to me and embraced me. They held me for a good long minute. My sobs rippled out; they sobbed along with me. In that collective embrace, in that moment, we were one organism, one soul. I was part of them, and they were part of me. I was welcome. I was loved.

Even though we all partied long into the night that night, all I thought about was that this was going to end. I'd just experienced what real belonging was, and I had to leave, and I didn't know how to carry this enormous warmth home with me.

WHEN WE ARRIVED back in Toronto, I had to separate from the rest of the company and board a flight back to Saskatoon. We said goodbye in the international terminal, hugging each other deeply, and I began walking to the domestic gates.

I didn't make it more than fifty feet before I realized how alone I was. The airport hallway was empty. I held myself against the wall; I found it difficult to breathe. My body felt empty, scoured clean. I gathered myself and found a place to sit, only to find myself fighting tears. I continued fighting them for hours, until I arrived back in Saskatoon. Keeping the tears down was like stuffing a cork in a volcano.

My wife picked me up at the airport. I hugged her, but I could barely speak. I waited until we got home.

I immediately ran down to the basement, locked the door behind me, and screamed. I screamed for ten minutes straight. I sobbed. I buckled on the floor. I let my wife in and told her everything. The city of Reims, the festival, and the play's company had formed the world's most wondrous incubator; I cried like a newborn, outraged at having been hauled out from its dark comforts but exhilarated at the astonishing and vivifying light of the world, within which it could flourish, if it chose.

Kai Cheng Thom

LANGUAGE IS THE FLUID OF OUR COLLECTIVE BODIES

Mother sings an old song in our ancestral language: *Yut moh, yut hoh, m'ang seen doh, yut moh yut san, m'ang se gan gan gan. Yut moh yut hoh, m'ang seen doh, yut moh yut san, m'ang se gan gan gang an. Yut moh yut hoh* . . . And over and over again. This is the song my mother sings when she is tending to a cut or a scrape, when she is applying lotion to the blisters and rashes of childhood. It is her healing song—at least, I think of it that way. I have a vague sense of the meaning as a whole—something about touch making the pain go away—but not the individual words.

Who knows where my mother got this song? Perhaps it is something ancient, from our *heng haa*, a place that is, for me, embedded in the bone of memory beyond time. Or maybe it's from a radio commercial. This isn't a language I speak, and I've accepted that it just won't be. I've been more ambitious from time to time, in the past—this language isn't dead after all, not with three million fluent speakers (according to Wikipedia, anyway) left in the world, though my research tells me that the majority of them are older. In a generation or two, its active use may be drastically reduced.

But there are no schools in North America that teach it, nor has there been any formal pedagogy developed around doing so, as far as I can tell. My ancestral language was not important enough for the Communist Party to actively destroy, but it was not important enough to save, either.

My sisters and I are all grown up now, so my mother almost never sings her healing song anymore.

MY ANCESTRAL LANGUAGE is not my mother tongue, exactly. "Mother tongue" implies complete fluency, doesn't it, not to mention a certain emotional ease? I know perhaps a hundred words in my ancestral language—though I am often able to mysteriously understand a good deal more—and I feel anything but ease with it.

English is my adopted mother tongue, I suppose, because I can do anything at all in English. Mama English bends to serve my every whim. *La belle français, elle m'aime bien aussi.* My ancestral tongue, though, is wilder, fiercer, eludes my attempts to dominate and conquer it. My ancestral language lives deep inside my body, a mostly dormant neural network, a vestigial organ that has lost its original purpose. It is a ghost limb; I still feel it trying to move, to break free, to carry out its purpose.

Sometimes I am embarrassed by my ancestral language, sometimes I like to indulge in the deep nostalgia that flows from my awareness of its presence. Most of the time, though, it's just there, a part of me I don't know what to do with. A ghost limb reaching back through time, trying to hold on to a place I've never been.

A CERTAIN TYPE of older, liberal, usually white Canadian likes to ask, "What kind of Chinese does your family speak? Cantonese or Mandarin?" They pride themselves on knowing that there is more than one kind of Chinese. They think it shows that they are not racist, they are not collapsing the entire global population of over one billion Chinese people into a homogenous mass. Unfortunately, they do not know that they have simply collapsed us into two homogenous masses instead.

I am not offended by this question—aren't we all ignorant to some extent about cultural experiences beyond our own? This is not an essay about political correctness but about longing. However, I am never sure how to answer because most of the people asking do not really want to know. It's like asking, "Are you okay?" of someone who has just gone through something difficult. It is a question that closes a door rather than opening one.

My mother speaks Cantonese (that is to say, the prestige Hong Kong dialect) fluently, though she has an accent, and it is not her mother tongue. My father says he speaks Cantonese fluently, but I realized a few years ago that this is somewhat boasting on his part because I asked him once to translate a Cantonese show that was playing on the TV, and he could not. This surprised me, because I have spent my whole life accompanying my father on trips to Cantonese-speaking businesses and Cantonese friends' homes, and he never seems to have a problem communicating. My father is one of those resilient immigrants you've heard so much about; he can grasp what is going on through context clues and camaraderie; he is clever and economical with the vocabulary he has, covering the gaps left by the words he doesn't.

I didn't understand what it meant to be highly conversational yet not fluent in a language until I moved to Quebec and learned to speak French. There are many tenses and idioms that escape me, but I know enough words in every category to stumble through a discussion of basically any topic, from food to health care to municipal governance. In fact, I can string sentences together so quickly and fluidly that native speakers at first often mistake me for a fluent speaker. It isn't until we are four or five sentences in that I see the light change in their eyes, the subtle condescension, as they begin to see the textures of my limitations, and this frustrates me because they do not know how intelligent I am in English. Is this how my father feels in Cantonese?

My father's and mother's most fluent language is English, but their emotional language is our ancestral tongue: this is the language that they speak to each other affectionately in, that they admonish us with, that they speak to each other when they want to keep secrets. My parents, both survivors of neglect and abuse and poverty and racism, carry the weight of the past in their mother tongue, and they have passed this weight on to me, a grief that cannot speak its name.

TRAUMA, IN ITS MANY FORMS, is becoming a topic of increasing interest in both psychological and lay communities: intergenerational trauma, developmental trauma, collective trauma, spiritual trauma. Sociologist Kai Erikson asserts that *collective* trauma refers to a breaking of the bonds between members of a society, so that the group identity of that society is fractured, thereby compromising the capacity of its members to relate to one another in an emotionally fluent way. Intergenerational trauma is the passing on of pain from one generation to the next, a transmission of the past that replicates itself over and over again. Spiritual trauma is a shattering of expectations about the meaning of human life, a rupture between our selves and the moral laws we once thought ordered the universe.

Studies of intergenerational trauma have shown that the children of survivors of terrible events often experience psychological and emotional pain similar to that of their parents—even when their parents have refused to discuss their traumas within the family. The story of what happened is still felt transmitted through the body and the mind even if it is not verbally spoken; studies have shown that trauma can be passed on epigenetically. The story of *what happened* writes itself into our DNA, even if we cannot read it.

I believe that language is the fluid within the collective body: like plasma, like blood, like spinal fluid, it carries nutrients and information from one unit to the next. Without the lubricating, life-giving qualities of language shared over time, the tissues of our relationships become tough and unresponsive. Our wounds fail to heal, we scarify and ossify. Something gets lost in the space between.

So you see, this is what I think about when I think about the fact that my paternal grandfather—whom I knew all my life until his death, and with whom I never had a single real conversation—was once imprisoned by the Japanese during World War II. Or when I think about my maternal grandmother, who moved to rural Canada in the 1950s and promptly developed a deep, decades-long psychosis. Or when I think about my great-grandfather, who, as the story goes, came to Canada in the early twentieth century as a labourer and was required to pay the head tax.

AS A DIASPORIC Chinese "Canadian" writer, I find myself tired of talking and reading about the head tax, though the truth is that even among the handful of other Chinese Canadian writers I know, there are very few whose family lineages actually stretch back to someone who was impacted by the Sinophobic Canadian policies of the early to mid-twentieth century. I think sometimes there is a certain impulse to bring up the head tax, the Exclusion Act, the racist burnings of Chinatowns as a precursor to diasporic Chinese North American literatures. It's as though we feel we need to justify talking about ourselves in a time when racist policy and culture is impacting others in much more urgent and vicious ways.

My angst around language is not, to me, an "important" issue in the sense of world politics—at this point in my life, it feels uncomfortably like navel-gazing. Chinese diasporic literatures sometimes feel to me like they are stuck in time, unable to move beyond the frozen alienation that is inherent in anti-Asian racism: perpetual outsiders and foreigners, always observers, and never a part of the cultural conversation. Our history and struggles are, I have found, opaque to non-Asians across the political spectrum; there is the sense that Chinese and broader Asian political experiences are not fully legible through colonial North American lens.

For some time, I considered this illegibility unimportant as well, until I recently remembered something I have learned in my studies of trauma therapy: it is the *whole* body's experience of living with trauma rather than the *isolated* experience of a trauma symptom that holds the key to healing. We need to understand the whole of our relationship to trauma in order to release it.

What does it mean when a society contains parts it is unable to read, refuses to understand? What happens to a society full of voices that it refuses to hear?

I DID NOT KNOW there was more than one kind of Chinese for the first several years of my life. In fact, I did not know there was more than one kind of non-white person; in my little world, there were Chinese people and English people, and it seemed clear to me that English people were superior. After all, the books and TV and menus and pretty much everything else were in English, while Chinese was just a weird language that my parents and old people spoke. Yet I also felt a deep shame for my inability to speak Chinese well, because I knew that Chinese fluency was something my parents expected of me as a way of honouring them. The notion of a more complex hierarchy was yet to come.

I started Chinese school when I was five, and I was already dreading it because I knew I wouldn't be able to match my older sister's stellar performance. Still, upon my arrival, I was shocked to discover that I had apparently somehow regressed from simply speaking Chinese badly to not speaking Chinese at all. The teachers, all fierce former schoolteacher ladies from Hong Kong, barked orders at me that were entirely incomprehensible. The other children all seemed to follow along perfectly well (I later learned this was because they were migrant children who already spoke Chinese fluently but were there to learn how to write). I was treated as the classroom dunce, denounced by the teachers and ostracized by the other students.

One evening at Chinese school, I drank too much water at break and developed an urgent need to go to the bathroom. I put up my hand and asked the teacher if I could go. She snapped something back at me, the gist of which, I gathered, was that she didn't know what I was saying. This perplexing phenomenon—that my Chinese teachers didn't understand even the Chinese words I thought I knew—was by now familiar to me, so I put down my hand and sat squirming in my seat. Humiliation and shame burned hot within my skin... and then, horror of horrors, burned hot outside my skin as well, soaking my cotton sweatpants, socks, and shoes. The stench of my stupidity and incapacity wafted through the air, alerting everyone in the classroom to my state, resulting in my prompt ejection and a furious call to my parents.

Many years later, I came to realize that the reason for the apparent, abrupt decline of my Chinese-language ability was that the language taught at my Chinese school was not, in fact, the language my family spoke at home, but rather the prestige dialect of Cantonese. When I asked my parents why they hadn't told me, they said they had thought the situation was too complicated to explain to a child.

A *somatic* perspective holds that trauma is a compulsive repetition of an embodied survival strategy; the unconscious mind, perceiving an existential danger, throws the body into a state of somatic reactiveness, releasing an animal response intended to remove the threat.

This is why survivors of violence might scream and lash out wildly in their sleep, why survivors of car accidents might compulsively vomit at the sight of an automobile, why people who have lived through painful situations from which they could not escape might experience a violent trembling in their legs—as if to flee—every time they are afraid. The bodily responses propelled by a trauma are compulsive, uncontrollable, often mysterious, as they respond to a logic—a language—that does not originate in the rational mind.

I did not know all this when I was five, however, so it was with renewed bewilderment and terror that I compulsively wet my pants every week in Chinese school for the next several weeks.

CANTONESE, *GUANGDONGHUA*, IS a sister language to my *heng haa hua*, my ancestral tongue; they are both a part of the Yue family of Chinese languages and are somewhat mutually intelligible. Mandarin, *Putonghua*, on the other hand, comes from a separate language family and is not mutually intelligible with the Yue Chinese varieties.

My *heng haa hua* was once the lingua franca of the overseas Chinese diaspora, and it still shows in the demographic composition of Chinatowns around the world today. Yet my *heng haa hua* was increasingly displaced in Canada by the arrival of *Guandonghua* Cantonese speakers as the handover of Hong Kong from Britain to the People's Republic of China became a reality.

Hong Kong Cantonese has enjoyed the status of a prestige dialect over the past century, thanks to the wealth and prominence of Hong Kong as an international business centre and former titan of soft cultural power in Asia. Hong Kong cinema, television, newspapers, and Cantopop all established Hong Kong *Guangdonghua* as an important language, with this ripple effect extending across oceans: my father still sounds bitter sometimes as he tells me that he wanted my sisters and me to learn Cantonese because the people from Hong Kong used to laugh at his accent. My mother became fluent in Cantonese to enhance her business as a family doctor, a strategy that has served her well late into her career.

But language, like politics and power, flows and ebbs in many directions at once. Even as Cantonese media proliferated, *Putonghua* was becoming established as the preferred language of the Communist Party, to the point of being inscribed as "Standard Chinese" worldwide. Over the next generation, Mandarin *Putonghua* was instated as the language of instruction in Chinese schools, as well as the dominant language in media; all other forms of Chinese were lowered to the status of "dialect" and were even scorned as backward in certain Chinese-speaking societies.

For a while, *Guangdonghua* seemed immune to the decline impacting other Chinese "dialects," but over the past decade, Hong Kongers have expressed increasing concern over the potential loss of Cantonese as a regionally dominant language. More and more Hong Kong parents are choosing to raise and educate their children in Mandarin, so as to retain status and career advantage.

THE FIRST QUEER Chinese Canadian author I read was Larissa Lai, whose novel *Salt Fish Girl* contains a scene in which the protagonist, a queer Chinese girl whose journey takes her through space and time, is offered the opportunity to absorb a new language so she can survive, at the cost of losing her mother tongue. She agrees, and her mother language literally flows out of her in the form of urine, which she flushes down the toilet.

Collective trauma is a shared experience that is communicated through feeling, image, and memory, even when it is not spoken aloud.

IN MY MID-TWENTIES, I decided to take a continuing education course in Cantonese. I was immediately struck by the fact that the school, a well-known university in Toronto, offered a vast range of courses in Mandarin, but only a few in Cantonese. Furthermore, the Mandarin instruction went all the way from basic to fluency, while the Cantonese instruction only comprised the beginner level. Like my ancestral tongue, Cantonese seems to be fading from the diasporic consciousness in North America. I guess even the sister to my mother tongue, once so extravagantly robust, is past her prime. Cantonese is important enough that the Communists have made serious attempts to marginalize it within China by restricting its use in schools and media, but not so important that Westerners have any interest in learning it.

Upon entering the class, I was pleased to find that most of the students were second- or third-generation Chinese Canadians like me—all from similar backgrounds and experiences when it came to language learning. I was also pleased to discover that I was often the class star: as it turns out, I remember more Cantonese than I thought.

One teacher, though, found it necessary to repeatedly correct my pronunciation of certain syllables, which I always seem to twist in a certain way. Over and over, I made this mistake. Finally, the teacher asked me, "What language did you speak at home?" I told her the name of my *heng haa hua*, and she said, "Of course! I thought so. This is why you have that kind of accent."

Trauma is sometimes thought of as a type of psychological scarring, a malformation of memory that forms around a distinctive shape. This memory marks itself deep in our embodied selves, becoming a part of the shape of our *somas*, our living body-minds. Post-traumatic growth is the experience of increased depth and meaning in life that sometimes results from exposure to traumatic wounding.

IF YOU ARE a certain kind of Chinese person, a scholar of Chinese history, or perhaps a linguist, you already know the name of my *heng haa hua*. Perhaps reading this has imparted another dimension of its meaning to you, or perhaps you have found some piece of yourself here in this essay, in the ghost of a vestigial organ. Diasporic literature is, of course, obsessed with ghosts and hauntings, with the homeland and the shape of the past, in a way that the writing of those who stayed in the mother country never seem to be.

And if you are any other type of reader, chances are you still don't know what my ancestral language is. Perhaps you would like to know. However, I must refuse to tell you, because this is not an essay about names or the politics of identity that are so popular today, and that cry out for the specificity and rage that is inherent in the naming of things. This is an essay about longing, and about memory, about grief over things that are not important enough for the world to talk about, and what it means to feel deeply for a thing you have no words to describe.

Somewhere in the body of this essay, there is a healing song we were meant to understand.

Sigal Samuel

LOVE AND OTHER IRREGULAR VERBS

I. My dad speaks ten languages

No, really, he does. In order of acquisition, they are:

1. English
2. French
3. Hindustani
4. Arabic
5. Hebrew
6. Mughrabi
7. German
8. Latin
9. Greek
10. Japanese

I should probably explain that my dad is the professor type. His specialty is mastering foreign languages—the more arcane, the better. If you ask him, he'll tell you he does this in order to be able to read the Great Books of Human Civilization in their original, unadulterated forms. If you ask me, though, he picked up half these languages to gain access to the women he loved, and whom—given enough practice with participles, plosives, and possessive pronouns—he might persuade to love him back.

II. Hum tumku boht pyar karta

My dad was born to Jewish but secular parents in 1950s Montreal. As a result, bilingualism was a given: he grew up immersed in both English and French. He also grew up surrounded by the strange sounds of his great-grandmother's patois—a peculiar blend of Arabic and Hindustani words. Granny was a Baghdadi Jew who had immigrated to India in her youth, caught the eye of a rich Bombay businessman, and stayed there to raise her brood. She spoke Arabic because that was the language of Baghdad, and Hindustani because that's what her Indian servants spoke.

My father was fascinated by Granny. Unlike his own meek mother, Granny was a tough old broad, a pigheaded matriarch who was always bursting into your kitchen, tasting whatever was simmering on the stove, and proclaiming, "Too much *haldi*! Too little *cotmeer*!" He was enthralled by the movement of her gnarled hands as she spoke, cutting through the air like branches in a windstorm; he was in love with her way of chewing tobacco and spitting into the spittoon with a soft *tu-tu-tu*! He wanted desperately to hear her stories of India—supposedly she'd owned a pet monkey, a baby leopard, and a goat named Peter—but of course she spoke no English and refused to learn.

So one day my father approached his mother, who (as she tells it) was washing dishes at the time, and begged her to teach him Arabic and Hindustani.

"One phrase every day," he pleaded.

"Shouldn't you be focusing on your schoolwork?"

"I want to talk to Granny," he insisted.

She studied his stubborn little face for a minute before agreeing. "Here's your first lesson. Go and tell Granny: *hum tumku boht pyar karta.*"

Obediently, he shuffled off and told her. Her face lit up; she kissed him on the crown of his head and sighed a soft *tu-tu-tu!* He returned to his mom and asked, "What does that mean?"

She said, "I love you very much."

III. Mazel Tov!

At around age seventeen, my father began to take a serious interest in Judaism. A social isolate from pre-K onward, he found himself hungry for some form of authentic connection—preferably one that didn't involve fraternizing with the stoner kids at Wagar High— and religion seemed to offer just that. After his first year of university, he dropped out and announced that he was going to live in Jerusalem, where he would study at an Orthodox yeshiva and learn how to live an observant Jewish life.

As it turns out, a big part of living an observant Jewish life in that setting meant, well, finding an observant Jewish wife. *How hard can it be?* thought my father, who'd never even had a girlfriend, never mind a potential life partner. It turned out to be harder than he'd thought. In the end, the head rabbi of his yeshiva appointed a matchmaker to help him find that special someone.

The story of how my father met my mother is one he often used to tell me as a bedtime story when I couldn't get to sleep. It runs a bit like Goldilocks and the Three Bears. The matchmaker showed up at his door on three separate occasions, each time with a different candidate in tow.

Candidate #1 was a Yemenite Israeli with big bones and an even bigger personality. She scared my father half to death, raining questions down upon him like burning sulphur on Sodom and Gomorrah. With each question his answers grew quieter and quieter, until he was speaking in a virtual whisper. Which, apparently, was a pet peeve of hers, because she proceeded to throw a fit right there in my father's living room. Too hot.

Candidate #2 was a wisp of a woman who looked like she could be blown off her perch if anyone so much as exhaled in her direction. She rivalled even my father in shyness and answered his questions in such delicate decibels that he couldn't make out her words. For the duration of the meeting he simply sat on the couch, looking at her and trying hard not to breathe. Too cold.

Candidate #3 was my mother. She was a pretty Moroccan girl with high cheekbones and sleek dark hair. She spoke at a normal volume and even made occasional eye contact. Her name, my father discovered with delight, was Mazel Tov—literally, good fortune. With a name like that, how bad a match could it be? After she'd left his apartment, he turned to the matchmaker and confided that he thought this last woman might be just right.

In the coming weeks, the matchmaker arranged a few more meetings between my father and mother. He travelled to Beit Shemesh, a town one hour outside Jerusalem, to meet her parents. Within seconds, my dad discovered that none of his languages—not even his fledgling Hebrew—would allow him to communicate with this wizened couple, who sat on their patio shrivelling in the sun like a pair of overripe prunes. They'd moved to Israel from a tiny village in Morocco and the language they spoke was a mash-up of Hebrew and Arabic known as Mughrabi. My father listened to their morphemes and phonemes clinking around in his ears and was charmed by their dialect as much as by their daughter. To this day, I'm convinced that his meeting with my mother's parents is what really cinched the deal. A new language was being offered up to him like a dowry.

Three months later, they were married. A few hours before the wedding night, the head rabbi of the yeshiva called my dad into his office and told him to take a seat. The old man then proceeded to give a strange demonstration: he brought his thumb and middle finger together in a loop and thrust the forefinger of his other hand in and out, in and out. Mortified, my dad realized that the rabbi was instructing him in the art of losing one's virginity. He was being subjected to the Orthodox version of sex ed.

For a couple of years, the marriage ran smoothly. My dad's Hebrew and Mughrabi improved dramatically. As time passed, though, his passion for the religious lifestyle began to wane. He started reading forbidden books—books his yeshiva deemed treif, intellectually unkosher. One day he picked up a copy of Nietzsche's *Beyond Good and Evil* and was captivated by the ideas he found in its pages. Soon enough the linguist in him emerged, demanding that he study German in order to read these texts in the original. And so he did. For the first time, a new language drove a wedge between him and the woman he loved.

IV. Être, Avoir, Aimer

After my parents split, my sister and I grew up with my dad in Montreal. As the male head of a single-parent household, he was sometimes at a loss for how to connect with two little girls. At a certain point, though, it occurred to him that he could use languages as a way of getting closer to us, just as he'd done with my great-great-grandmother and my mom. Other girls got dolls and dresses; we got diphthongs and dangling modifiers.

We already spoke English, of course, but no matter: when I was eight years old, my dad told my sister and me that he'd pay us a dime for every picture book we read and a quarter for every chapter book. We had to discuss the books with him before he'd pony up the cash. Budding entrepreneur that I was, I polished off entire series of books that year—*Nancy Drew, Boxcar Children, Goosebumps*—as fast as my money-grubbing paws could flip the pages.

When I reached Grade 2, my dad started helping me with my French homework. I still remember standing barefoot on the cold kitchen tiles and licking a cherry popsicle while he quizzed me on verb conjugation.

"*Je suis, tu es, il est,*" he declaimed, the *Bescherelle* propped open on his knees.

"*Nous sommes, vous êtes, ils sont!*" I recited between slurps on the popsicle.

"*J'ai, tu as, il a.*"

"*Nous avons, vous avez, ils ont!*"

"*J'aime, tu aimes, il aime,*" he said, and I froze, because the use of the first-person term of affection followed by a second-person pronoun was not something I was used to hearing. I looked down and saw that the popsicle was dripping onto my hand in sweet, sticky trails.

As a teen, I attended a Jewish high school where everyone had to learn Hebrew. I brought my homework into my dad's study sometimes, and even though by this point his bookshelves betrayed his atheist leanings, we worked on my Hebrew by studying the Bible together. Nietzsche and his giant moustache smiled down on us forgivingly.

By the time I became a student at McGill, I was still living at home, but my dad was spending more and more time cooped up in his study. Dictionaries encased him like a child's snow fort. As he sat poring over auxiliary verbs and adverbial clauses, I started to feel increasingly elided, like a weakly aspirated *h* at the beginning of a Greek word. So I did what I had to do to become audible: I enrolled in Arabic classes. I knew it would mean long afternoons of paging through the Arabic dictionary with him—and it did. By the end of my second year, I was wearing the gloss off its pages. The substance melted onto my hands, sweet and sticky. *Nous aimons, vous aimez, ils aiment.*

V. Tadaima

Earlier this year, my father met a woman on the internet. He lives in Montreal and she lives in Tokyo; they met in a chatroom. Started talking books. She's a comparative lit student. Japanese and English folktales or some such thing.

I live in Vancouver now, but my sister, who lives in downtown Montreal with her new husband, still goes over to our old house in the suburbs every Friday to have dinner with my dad. I get weekly phone calls from her, reporting on the status of his internet relationship. She says she can gauge how well it's going by the height of the pile of Japanese language books on his desk. Ten books or less means it's just a crush; twenty means it's getting serious; thirty or more and they're in love.

A week before I was due to fly home for winter break this year, my dad taught me the Japanese phrase *Tadaima*, which means "I'm home!" Sure enough, that's what I said when I turned my key in the lock and stepped back into the house I grew up in. Before he could even respond with the traditional rejoinder (*Okaeri*, which means "Welcome home!"), my eyes landed on the Jenga tower of Japanese books he'd just gotten out of the library. That's when the question popped into my head: does my dad learn foreign languages to gain access to women he loves, or is falling in love an excuse for him to learn another language? Either way I looked at it, the answer was yes.

To be with my great-great-grandmother, my dad learned Arabic and Hindustani. To be with my mother, he learned Hebrew and Mughrabi. Now, to be with his internet girlfriend, he's learning Japanese.

To be with me, my dad tried to learn the language of tenderness, of fatherly affection, but he stumbled over its intimate grammar, how to conjugate *to love* and other irregular verbs like *to miss a daughter without making her feel guilty for leaving home and to not live in a fort made of dictionaries*. I think, now, that I can spot the source of his trouble: his love for language grew so strong that it began to strangle the human love it was meant to nourish, the same way an umbilical cord can asphyxiate a baby on its way out of the birth canal.

VI. I speak five languages

Well, almost. I'm still working on number five. In order of acquisition, they are:

1. English
2. French
3. Hebrew
4 Arabic
5. Spanish

Four of these five languages, I learned in order to get closer to my dad. One of these languages, I learned in order to distinguish myself, to set myself apart.

This summer, I started learning Spanish. On the first day of class, our teacher, Enrique, taught us how to say "I love you." *Te amo.* Strangely, my first thought was: as in ammo? Like, ammunition? My second thought was: oh, of course, *amo* as in *amour.* Enrique quickly moved on to the verb *hablar,* to speak. He asked us to open our Spanish textbooks to the appropriate page and began leading the class in a resounding chorus of *yo hablo, tu hablas, el habla* blah blah— I stopped listening. I was thinking about how there was something right in that first thought, in that etymology that linked love with ammunition, with warfare. Beneath my palm the textbook radiated heat, full of plosives preparing to detonate at the slightest pressure from my tongue.

Rebecca Fisseha

SAY SOMETHING IN YOUR LANGUAGE

ong before I began writing creatively in English, I knew that the
status quo for non-English words in an English text was italici-
zation. This convention always popped me out of the reading
experience and made me feel distanced as a reader. An experience
that was worsened, of course, if the non-English word in question
was from the Amharic language, my mother tongue. Although I
accepted the situation, I think as a writer I subconsciously avoided it.
I wrote plays, short stories, and articles for several years before I was
ever faced with the need to italicize anything, which was when I
started writing my novel *Daughters of Silence*. Perhaps because of the
length of the project, it was finally time to confront the issue.

Initially, I followed the status quo and italicized the Amharic words.
But I also checked how other Ethiopian diaspora writers writing in
English—for a mainstream audience of Western anglo readers, for the
most part—handled this issue. Among the books I inspected were
How to Read the Air by Dinaw Mengestu, *Beneath the Lion's Gaze* by

Maaza Mengiste, and *Notes from the Hyena's Belly* by Nega Mezlekia. Their choices varied. Some had only one or two Amharic words in an entire novel, which were italicized. Others had a lot more, also italicized. Their generosity with explanations or descriptions for the reader also varied, but none left the reader totally high and dry.

For the most part, though, they chose the English equivalent (which, of course, is never truly equal), either because that was their preference or because there is no direct translation. But readers who will notice the discrepancy, no matter how tiny, because they know both languages, are in the minority and are used to worse discrepancies in life.

For myself, I found that italicizing didn't sit well with me. Neither did using equivalents, nor offering some level of explanation. I wanted to find a way to get rid of this distancing effect that all those choices created, both for readers who do, and do not, know Amharic.

The worst offenders were italics, of course. Italics warn the latter kind of reader that a "foreign" word is coming up, since italics are easily spotted by a glance at a page. Such a reader then comes at the text already with their guard up, and the immersive experience is disrupted. For the former kind of reader, those who do know said language, in this case Amharic, the distancing is magnified. They are already making a concession by reading in English, living in English, and then there's this. They are being given something they don't need. Unnecessary special delivery.

My solution, to get rid of this distancing problem, was to fiddle with Amharic and see if I could inject as much of it into English as possible, to create as immersive an experience for everyone, within the confines of the language I had to use. This fiddling with Amharic, both for creative purposes and just for fun, was something I began doing when I became interested in my own culture again in early adulthood. Around that time, the late nineties to the early aughts, this resurgence of reclaiming began with me hoarding everything and anything Ethiopian, especially Amharic words. I had notebooks of words, phrases, expressions, collected from the Amharic works I was reading and from everyday conversations. When I began to write, around the same time, it was initially for the theatre. I wrote in English but also in Amharic. My favourite thing to do was write experimental monologues in Amharic—messing around with meanings, coming up with abstract stuff. Then in grad school, I wrote a literal and interpretive translation of five chapters from the classic novel *Fikir Iske Meqabir* by Haddis Alemayehu as my thesis project, which was entitled *Translation as Experience*.

By the time *Daughters of Silence* was taking shape, I decided that instead of dancing around dealing with language in the novel by poking at Amharic, I should go to the source, as they say, talk to the experts, collect original textbooks, find out how Amharic works syntactically, grammatically, look at the inner workings of something I had never had to consciously learn except for reading and writing.

I said as much in my OAC Chalmers Fellowship grant application, and the jury agreed. One of the outcomes of that research in Ethiopia, the UK, and the US was that I further developed something I had decided to call Amharglish. It was beyond just "broken English." I transposed (tried to) the rules of Amharic syntax and grammar, as much as I had managed to learn in six months, onto English. Then I used that "language" to write about a third of the novel from the point of view of a central character who spoke only Amharic and had lived in Ethiopia all her life.

The problem was that readability went out the window. Amharglish was a cool, bizarre, freakish thing, magic for grant applications, and made for a great conversation topic, but it was a disaster to understand. I had overcorrected for the problem. Even Amharic speakers would have trouble deciphering the text, just like my experimental Amharic monologues had left some people in the community scratching their heads.

It was time for another decision. Do I want to create books people read or abstract experimental curiosities for six academic people to "study"? So I shaved down this Amharglish to only appear in the dialogue of certain characters, and then took even that away, trusting that the reader will understand that the characters are not speaking English even though what they say is written in English. After all, I'd been doing that as a reader all my life.

As for the eighty-four words that had to be in Amharic, I told myself to stop trying to reinvent the wheel and get over it and use the damn italics. At this point, my agent and I were sending out the manuscript of *Daughters of Silence* to publishers. I was even open to the idea that a glossary might be a part of the published book. Though the notion of a novel with a glossary gave me twitches, because it was such a rude yanking-out of the reader from the imaginary world of the story.

In the meantime, there was a shift in the literary conversation among bilingual writers, a vocal opposition to this italicizing business. I remember a video made by a Daniel José Older, a Latinx writer, in response to a question he gets a lot: "Why don't you italicize non-English language use in the text?" In the video, he starts his response by way of an example sentence, which he begins speaking in English, dressed in a plain T-shirt. Then he cuts to impersonating his version of a stereotypical Latinx dude—cigar, fancy hat, shirt open to an undershirt exposing hairy chest loaded with chains—just to say a single word in Spanish. Then he then cuts back to himself in his T-shirt, continuing the sentence in English. He does this to give a visual demonstration, a very effective one, of how comical it is to italicize, concluding, "That's not what happens. That's not what we sound like. That's not what anybody sounds like."

The solution was, of course, don't italicize. Embed the foreign words in the same font as the English words, because that is a true reflection of reality. Like those moments when, by pure accident, an

Amharic word barges in while I'm speaking to a monolingual person in English, or how I naturally mix languages when I'm speaking to an English-Amharic bilingual person. Or when I'm on the receiving end of such moments from bilingual speakers of other languages. It's all the lived version of non-italicizing. As in, it's life. You surmise the meaning or you don't. Either way, you suck it up and move along.

But I had never experienced it as a reader. Until I finally did, and loved it. Now it seems like an obvious thing that shouldn't have taken me so long to realize. It helped that my first experience of this way of writing was not just any book but one that had done well critically and commercially, and that I actually liked a lot. It was *The Best Place on Earth* by Ayelet Tsabari. Because there wasn't that "Warning: Foreign Word Ahead!" signal of italics, I got to stay immersed in the world of the stories. Yet I wasn't completely left out as a reader, because I gathered enough meaning from the context. And I appreciated the slight delay, the hiccup in the flow of English going on in my brain while I read. That was as it should be. The full meaning of a word or phrase in Hebrew should forever evade me because Hebrew isn't "mine."

I decided to emulate that approach. By then I had a publisher. So I waited for pushback. I had a defence ready. I was going to say, "Hey, listen, there are already lots of quotes and text messages and inscriptions in italics in this novel. It will be too much if every transliterated Amharic word, of which there are almost a hundred, is italicized."

Nobody blinked. Nobody said boo. More proof that attitudes really were changing. I hoped that just as I had appreciated the non-italicized words, so would my readers, and they would see that, rather than taking away from their reading experience, it may enhance it. Or at least they'd be okay to go along with it and not begrudge me the little bit of extra work they have to do as readers, that they wouldn't mind staying on the other side of a little gap that would never close.

Of course, I still sprinkled, in one or two places, text in Ge'ez script. Doesn't hurt anybody, I thought. I couldn't help a nod to the original. If a reader understands it, it would feel like a little hug, to make up for having to read our mutual experience in English at all. If a reader didn't understand it, they just have something pretty to look at.

The response from early and later readers was good, even yeah-what's-the-big-deal casual. Granted, it's only been a year since publication at the time of this writing. People have so far understood the rationale, except for those who haven't. One individual sent me an email complaint, a request that I justify the profusion of Amharic words. The message was along the lines of "Why did you do this to me, when I had been so good to buy your book and read it through and deem it 'superb'? Why did you make me, who already has an expert knowledge of several Eastern languages, have to look stuff up?"

I will let this essay be my response. To say, "I'm not doing it 'to' you, I'm doing it 'for' you." You've taken the non-italicizing, the non-explaining, as an aggression, as an act of exclusion. But it's my way, the best way I've found to include you, to keep you as close as possible. Besides, while we're on the topic, the few minutes of inconvenience you suffered as a reader are nothing compared to having to live your whole life this way. Not because there are too many words you don't understand, but because you understand all the words of all the languages you use, yet still feel distanced.

Add to that being asked, now and then, to actually italicize yourself, simply for someone's entertainment. I'm sure anyone who is bilingual, especially of a non-European heritage, is used to being asked, "Say something in your language!" It's not up there with the "Where are you from?" moment, but it should be. Of course, the asker may be after more than just entertainment, let's give them some credit. They may genuinely believe they will get an unfiltered, authentic version of you. A shortcut, if you will, to the soul of a person. But no matter the intent of the asker, to me, such a request widens, not lessens, the gap because meaning is not carried across at the same moment of utterance, or even later, in translation.

Rarely, the gap between people is lessened, though it does happen. Such moments are as beautiful as they are totally unplannable.

It was the morning after, and he was driving me home. During our get-to-know-you-now-that-I've-slept-with-you chit-chat, he asked the inevitable.

"Say something in your language."

"What do you want me to say?"

That's always my go-to response. Even though I know the "something" doesn't matter. The asker wants to be tickled, and in his case I didn't mind obliging. At all.

"I don't know."

So I said, "አላውቅም."

"What does that mean?" he said.

"I don't know."

"You don't?"

"No, it means 'I don't know,'" I said.

"Say it again?"

"Alawkim."

"I like him?"

"No," I said, and laughed. He was wrong. I was lying. And somewhere in there we'd managed to understand each other perfectly.

I do concede that, compared to creative writers from the Ethiopian diaspora whose work I know, I have quite a lot of Amharic words in *Daughters of Silence*. I think, in my heart of hearts, I secretly just wish I could have written the whole thing in Amharic and still had it perfectly understood, somehow, like that moment above. To use your own language and have all your meanings, conscious and unconscious, intended and unintended, be understood—that is the ultimate dream.

Logan Broeckaert

GENDER FLUENT

drummed my fingers on the arm of the chair while I waited for my doctor to come back with a printed copy of my antidepressant prescription. I had let him remind me that it was a good sign that my mood was stable, tell me my next Pap test was due in March, and confirm that all my immunizations were current, while I choked on the words I had practised for months. I felt like my mother at the end of her illness, when the only language she had was thick and guttural.

When he came back, I stood up to take the sheet of paper from him and rush-whispered before I lost my nerve, "Can I—Do you— What's the process for top surgery?"

"Like, generally?" he asked.

"Yes," I said, "but no. I mean, I want it for me."

"I'm not sure we've ever talked about this." My doctor searched my face for an answer, and I felt chastened like I was incorrect, invalid, insufficient, like already I wasn't enough. "There's an assessment," he said. "Book an appointment, we'll have a chat, and then I'll recommend the surgery."

I didn't trust my mouth so I nodded instead.

THE VILLAGE I GREW UP in was small, so small that I knew everyone up and down every street and on every unpaved back road. Then, *queer* was the slur we used for the Anglican minister with the perfect gardens, for the swishy handyman with the neat beard, for the melancholic drunk at my dad's bar who always tucked in his shirt. We used it to shame gay people but we also used it to affirm our and others' straightness, whether we were straight or not.

I moved to Toronto in my twenties, and a colleague at one of my first jobs mentioned being queer, and I heard the word differently than I had ever heard it before. The way he had said it, leaning against my cubicle wall, was warm and gentle; he made it sound so vast I was sure it could hold anything, like all the ways my sexual orientation, gender expression, and gender identity had veered away from cis hetero norms. I took it for myself.

I considered the meaning of other words, how I might reclaim them, and use them to build a lexicon of the self. I tried gay lady, househusband, auntie, sibling, boyfriend, guy, woman, little sister, daughter, to see how they fit. As a masc person with a female body who didn't identify exclusively with either gender, it was important to me to find a language that didn't sit heavy on my tongue. I told straight friends that I learned how to be a good boyfriend from their complaints about their failed relationships. I queered gendered language, changed its meaning to suit me. I asked Frances how she liked having a househusband who did her laundry and made her lunch. I told my sister how I missed being someone's daughter since our mom died, held tight to the word *daughter*, even as a trans masculine person, because it is how my mother had known me.

DURING THE ASSESSMENT I kept my eyes on my feet, then I stared straight ahead. Even though my doctor had already said he would recommend me for surgery, I felt I had to perform for him. Knowing the outcome of the assessment gave me the feeling of having been given something I had better show I deserved.

I checked the industrial clock with the red second hand like a third grader on a Friday afternoon in late spring. My doctor kept asking open-ended questions, which I answered as narrowly as possible. There was an entire gender-neutral language available to me to make this performance a good one. I could tell the doctor I used they/them pronouns, show him I knew how to say chest instead of breasts, let him see all the ways I could scrub gender from my lexicon when I needed to. I had experience with this type of performance: I grew up an anglophone kid in Quebec. I had used my fluent French for years to demonstrate my worth to people with the power to give me the things I needed.

But I wasn't fluent in gender-neutral language when talking about myself and I didn't want to rely on the gendered language I had become so comfortable with, in case it gave my doctor the impression that I didn't need this surgery. Instead, I told the doctor what I knew, which was that my breasts had always seemed wrong on my body. As a teenager, I wrapped them tightly in sports bras. As an adult, I bound them. I told him this discomfort with my breasts had gotten worse as I got older. I told him I wasn't interested in hormones, that I didn't feel like a man. He typed as I talked, translated what I said into the clinical language he preferred. "So, it sounds like you've been experiencing dysphoria for a long time now."

WHEN I WAS FIFTEEN, I told my mom I was gay in the family minivan as we both stared straight ahead at the cornstalks, beige and frost-bitten, in the snow-covered fields. I said, "I know I'm gay." I couldn't explain how I knew or what it meant specifically for me, just that I knew I didn't like boys. Briefly, I hoped the gayness would go away, but when it didn't I accepted it, and over a number of years, started telling people. Most people, if we talked about it at all, used lesbian to describe me even though I had been careful to avoid it.

I didn't like the way lesbian sounded like a disease out of my mouth, the way it came off my mother's tongue like an insult, the way kids at my school sharpened it to lezzie and used it as a weapon. I didn't know I could ask people to use the language I had chosen—what teenager knows they have the right to ask something like that?—so they said lezzie and lesbian and homo and dyke and muff diver and carpet licker. I couldn't control what people said or whether they said it with respect or disgust. These others, most of whom knew I was gay—my classmates, my colleagues, my friends, my family—didn't use the word I had chosen, so I stopped naming myself for straight people who did not need to name themselves for me.

"HAVE YOU TRANSITIONED socially?" the doctor asked. Had I, for example, come out to my friends and family as trans? Had I changed my pronouns? I didn't have a coming-out story that was neat and practised. I couldn't point to an email I had sent to my friends and family or a confession to Frances. I hadn't announced a transition to anyone because I didn't see surgery as a transition at all. It was just the next way I wanted to embody myself. I never talked about it like it was the end or the beginning of anything.

The doctor waited for an answer. "I haven't come out," I said. "And I'm ambivalent about my pronouns." He typed this into the form on the compufer screen. "I use the word *genderqueer* sometimes," I added, but it felt like I hadn't gone far enough. "I guess I'm non-binary." It sounded like something he could write in my assessment, something that would prove my case.

A FEW DAYS after surgery, I FaceTimed my brother. He answered from his recliner; his face—angled so low I was looking up his nose—filled the screen. We had planned this call earlier in the day because my niece had a few questions. He flipped the camera so I could see her. She wanted to know if she should call me uncle now.

There was a kid in Stanbridge East, a few years younger than I was, who had mixed up *uncle* and *aunt* when she was first learning to talk. This kid, and all the kids who came after, called their aunt Uncle Shelley. I thought about Shelley as I looked at Ayla's earnest expression. She was growing up in Stanbridge East—a place where *queer* was still an insult—and yet here she was, aged eleven, asking about the language I wanted her to use.

I didn't want to be called uncle. I hadn't known my own uncles well but I remembered feeling close to and cared for by two of my mother's sisters. My aunts had been comfortable substitutes when my mom was away. "I want you to keep calling me auntie," I said to Ayla. I wanted to be the warmth for her that my aunts had been for me.

IN SUMMER, AFTER SURGERY, as I started to feel looser in my body, the trouble I had had talking about myself in the doctor's office came back. Gendered language became insufficient for the meaning I needed it to convey. I worried that saying *gay lady* or *little sister* or *daughter* gave permission to others to avoid acknowledging my transness. I worried I wasn't trans enough because I wasn't changing my pronouns. I got sullen and awkward, suddenly a thirty-five-year-old boy with a real fear that my voice would crack any time I opened my mouth. It made conversations so hard, I talked less. When I did talk, I was hesitant and vigilant.

In early fall, in a conversation with Frances about a condescending window salesman who came to our house and patronized us, I asked, "Do you think he treated us like that because—" But then I stopped. What I wanted to say was "because two women live here?" but instead I said, "Because no men live here?" and it sounded like I was hiding something, and I hated it.

THAT WINTER, I LAY AWAKE in bed, hands on my flat chest, and considered whether it was time to become fluent in gender-neutral language, to deepen the well of words I was willing to use to describe myself. I thought about a podcast I heard about how some communities in Hawaii were trying to save Hawaiian through proven language-learning strategies. I wondered if I could use self-talk, a practice where learners have conversations with themselves, to become fluent.

I had imaginary conversations about hypothetical people whose faces I never bothered to fill in. I said *person, kid, parent, sibling, partner, spouse*—any word that left gender out. English was easy that way—there was always a word, you just needed to find it. I practised using *they/them* pronouns to talk about animals and objects and bus drivers and the people who picked up our recycling.

I tripped over and over again, caught myself, and kept practising. When I starting using gender-neutral language in conversation with others, it came out so smooth, like I was a native speaker, but it felt conspicuous, like I was yelling in these mostly cis hetero spaces whose members—my colleagues, my friends, my family—held tightly on to gendered language. I worried people thought I was patronizing them or performing wokeness. It made me feel out of place, like when I first moved to Montreal for university with my provincial accent. I had scrubbed my mouth of that accent, making room for a new one to take hold. I couldn't do that this time. I needed gender-neutral language as much as I needed gendered language. They had to learn to coexist.

IN SPRING, I WAS confined to my house and its back garden, and Frances was the only person I talked to because of the pandemic. For almost a year, I had spoken guardedly. As I settled into gender-neutral language, I learned it too was too small for the meaning I needed it to convey. Quarantine gave me the opportunity to practise using gendered language again safely, to gain back my confidence, to build back my lexicon.

In a way, I was six again, learning how to be bilingual. My mother sent my siblings and me to French school so we could flourish in the dominant language of our home in a way that she never could. I learned French at school and spoke English at home. For the first few years, I often struggled to find the right word in either language for a feeling or object or concept. Then I worried I was becoming untethered from English, the only language my mother knew. I was frustrated when, mid-sentence, I would have to switch from English to French to say le saut à la corde, as I pumped my arms around and around to show and tell my mom what I had done during recess because I couldn't find the word for skipping.

In quarantine, I struggled to find the right words because I was tentative and anxious, feeling out the possibilities in my mouth before I said them. And then, over the next few months, it was easy, like when I was nine and French and English finally settled and the words were there, and I had all the language I needed.

That spring, I was a gay lady, a daughter, a househusband, but also a sibling, a partner. I was less hesitant, less vigilant. I didn't need to worry whether people were taking me seriously as a trans person: there was only Frances, and she knew who I was.

Taslim Jaffer

HOW TO SAY BANANA IN KISWAHILI

"Which sufario should we make the soup in?" I asked my twelve-year-old daughter, Inaya, as she pored over the recipe for Chicken and Sweet Corn Soup on my iPhone. I held out two choices.

She shrugged and turned back to the list of ingredients. "I think we should use the bigger pot."

"Pot?" I said. "It's a sufario!"

She laughed. "It's a pot!"

I faked horror but I was gripped by a familiar, unsettling feeling. "Please, just say the word sufario. You know how to say it, you know what it means. Please use it!"

Inaya looked up. "Okay, Mom. It's a sufario." A silence hung over us. I pretended to move on from our conversation by pulling out the eggs we'd need to beat and add at the very end of the recipe.

Did Inaya concede and use the Kiswahili word because she recognized the importance of doing so or because she was avoiding a fifteen-minute lecture on her family's rich cultural-linguistic background? Did it even matter to her that her ancestors travelled by dhow on the monsoon winds across the Indian Ocean from Gujarat to East Africa, where generations of them tried to build a life? Was it at all interesting to her that even though socially the Asians and Africans were segregated, there was some adaptation of language in the intersections where people came together?

I glanced over at her. She placed the iPhone down on the island and turned to pull cans of creamed corn from the pantry. These questions were loaded and unfair; I kept them inside me, busying myself with the task of finding the can opener that always seemed to travel from drawer to drawer and was never where I had put it last.

Being from Mombasa, Kenya, right on the equator, I can't use the North American hyperbole: "Do you know your grandparents walked to school in the snow, uphill—both ways?" My equivalent is "Do you know your grandparents spoke five different languages?" Unlike my North American counterparts, I am not exaggerating; my parents speak Kutchi (our native regional language), Gujarati (our native state language), Kiswahili (from having grown up in Kenya), Hindi (from watching Bollywood movies), and English (the language of instruction in school). The Kutchi we speak now incorporates many Kiswahili words, a shift that began within a generation of living in East Africa. It was only when I pursued a minor in linguistics at university that I was able to tease apart the two languages. To this day, I blow my dad's mind when I say, "You know, that word you used isn't even Kutchi, it's Kiswahili." And when I ask him for the Kutchi word that was replaced, he is hard-pressed to find an answer.

My children can get away with speaking only English where we live, even within our family; there isn't a single relative now who doesn't speak it. They even use English to communicate with their ninety-seven-year-old great-grandmother who learned the language through the twisted, dramatic story plots of *General Hospital* when she moved to Canada in her fifties. But there is something about them only speaking English that doesn't sit well with me.

I worry that their monolingualism will erase where they came from.

This is something I have discussed with other parents who have the same cultural-linguistic background as me. Every so often, in a private Facebook group of local Ismaili moms, someone would post, seeking advice about passing down the language. The answer, of course, is providing as immersive an environment as possible.

This is not easy—with English now being my primary language, and the language I think in, it is a real effort to remember to use my mother tongue. When I started elementary school in Victoria, BC, there were many occasions when Kutchi or Kiswahili words would slip into my English sentences. I remember practising the difference between *tongue* and *thumb*, trying to produce the distinction between their initial sounds and figuring out where my tongue had to land while making them. Over time, English dominated my spaces—school, friends' homes, extracurricular activities—and eventually, though my parents continued to speak to me in Kutchi, I would reply in English. I maintained my first language because of my inter-actions with my two grandmothers, one of whom had never learned English. My husband only speaks English, as that was the common language between his Urdu-speaking mom and Kutchi-speaking dad. And so, it became our primary language.

As Inaya and I added garlic, ginger, and diced carrots to the sufario, I reflected on the many times my children have engaged with Kutchi or Kiswahili words effortlessly and felt my mood lift a little.

I remembered a familiar scene in which I have found myself with each of my three kids throughout their early years. We sat in a doctor's waiting room, with several other sniffling, coughing patients. The children's toy corner, decorated with Mother Goose nursery rhymes and separated by a faux-stone border like one you might find around a garden bed, was crawling with snot-nosed toddlers. I was prepared. I had a couple toys and books from home in my bag, ready to pull out when my own toddler's curiosity and boredom grew. The moment they wandered toward the germ-covered, half-dressed dolls in the shared play space, I said to them with a wide smile and a singsong voice: "Adeej ma. Chafu ai!" The other unsuspecting parents in the waiting room didn't realize I was forbidding my kids, in a combo of Kutchi and Kiswahili, to play with the same toys their kids were mouthing. And for that moment, I could pretend I was raising bilingual children.

I remembered when my nine-year-old son, Aariz, admitted that he only learned the English word *medicine* a couple years prior. Up until then, the word for any pharmaceutical or even vitamin was the Kutchi word dava. Every morning, my kids eat their C dava, D dava, and fishy dava.

I remembered that *laundry hamper* is foreign to my kids, doesn't feel right on their tongues. When their clothes are strewn across their bedroom floors, they know I'm going to be on them to put the dirty ones in the chafu kapada—chafu meaning dirty in Kiswahili and kapada meaning clothes in Kutchi.

I remembered when my five-year-old daughter, Alyzeh, had a school friend over, and her friend asked if she was having dinner at our place. "Not this time, sweetie. But maybe I can ask your mom if you can stay over another time?"

"Sure!" she responded, precociously. "And what kinds of things do you make for dinner?"

I paused, caught off guard by having to provide my culinary resumé to a kindergartner. "Well, I can make burgers or spaghetti or chicken..."

"And," Alyzeh piped up, proudly, "she can make macho ngombe!"

I beamed. Not only did my daughter know the colloquial way to ask for sunny-side-up eggs in Kiswahili but it was the *only* way she knew how to ask for it. One day, over brunch in a diner with friends, she'll order them in English, but these words will come to her mind first.

As for my kids being functionally fluent in the language of their ancestors, though, the chances are slim.

That's why I push for these phrases and words I know are a part of their lexicon. My English-only-speaking friends laugh when I lament that these scarce words include *armpit, underwear, fart*. "How?" I say to these friends who have never spent a day in their life thinking about passing down their native language. "How did I manage to teach them these random words but not anything that can form actual conversation?" They think it's hysterical that I ask my youngest daughter, "Did you wipe your bagals?" after her shower.

I'm not a purist by any means. I think language is exciting in the way it changes; the subsequent new words, and how they are used, tell interesting stories of human history.

For example, that word sufario? It's an adaptation.

It originates from the Kiswahili word 'sufaria' which means cooking pot. Kutchi households that employed native African housekeepers adopted this word (and many others) and then applied the linguistic rules of their own native tongue.

Kutchi has grammatical gender while Kiswahili does not. Somehow, *cooking pot* became masculine, which requires the suffix -*o*, and that's how sufario came to be.

My insisting that my children use this word might seem silly to my great-great-grandparents, who had never even heard of it. In fact, I don't know what word they would have used instead; it was one that was replaced.

When my dad moved in with us in the fall of 2019, the language differences among the three generations in my home became evident. By default, my dad speaks primarily our East African version of Kutchi with me. I like it. It makes me feel like I am in my own world with him, and it gives me a chance to practise. I have to think a little harder when conjugating certain verbs, reach deep into the language files in my brain to decide if something is masculine or feminine. Dad is patient. And speaking Kutchi with him feels like home, even as I hear my Canadian accent diluting the sounds.

TWO YEARS AGO, Inaya entered the Late French Immersion program and is already functionally fluent. Within months of being immersed in a French classroom, she was thinking in French. She will graduate from high school with a dual certificate, one in each of Canada's two official languages. I am pleased that she took this opportunity to stretch her brain in the way that language learning requires and that she enjoys the ease of slipping between tongues.

"I totally didn't even realize my teacher was speaking French when he was explaining the math to me!" she shared.

"That's so awesome!" I say, hugging her over this triumph.

The irony is not lost on me that her two languages are the colonial languages of this country and have nothing to do with our history. I swat at the pesky thought.

I have not stopped persisting, insisting they use as many of our native words as they know, providing as much exposure as I can give them in our day-to-day lives. Asking them in Kutchi what they want for breakfast. Holding up my fingers while asking, "Hakro ke ba?" to find out how many slices of toast they would like.

Maybe my kids will hear my voice in their head when they pull out a sufario from their own kitchen cupboards one day. Maybe they will use the word with their own kids or maybe they will simply think of it with fondness but not pass it down. How much further will this word reach?

These are some of the thoughts that come with motherhood for me. Passing down languages is not talked about on the playground or in parenting magazines as much as diaper brands and extracurricular activities and high school programs. Yet, for many first-generation Canadians it is an added dimension of parenthood. We try to pull our ancestry and culture and history into the here and now, at the kitchen island with our kids, so they can get a sampling— even just a taste—of where they come from, of all those generations that existed in other countries before coming to Canada.

ONE DAY, A FEW months after Dad moved in, he was chopping onions at the kitchen island. A couple tomatoes rested nearby, ready to be diced. To their right, the spice dabba was open. I knew he'd be dipping into the ground cumin, ground coriander, and turmeric once the onions were nicely browned. I'd grown accustomed to his rhythm when creating a masala base. I settled into a stool across from him and beside Inaya, who was absent-mindedly nibbling on an apple. Living with Dad means that whoever is in the kitchen, cooking, has the other's company. Sometimes dishes are created together, but usually, if he's at the helm, I'm happy to sit and talk his ear off.

I don't remember our conversation that day but I do know it was in Kutchi, and it was engrossing enough that I completely forgot Inaya was next to me. Inaya, who did not understand a word of what we were saying.

Suddenly, we were interrupted. "Ndizi!" Inaya called.

I laughed while Dad stopped chopping and stared at Inaya.

"I don't know what you guys are saying!" she said.

And so she had butted into the conversation with the first Kiswahili word that came to her mind. Banana.

Ashley Hynd

THE SEVEN GRANDFATHERS AND TRANSLATIONS

am sitting in the window of a cottage in the Muskokas watching snow fall softly through the trees, covering the still-frozen lake. Giizhik outside the window is taller than this two-storey home. She has likely seen countless generations claim this land. Watching her bow and bend to the wind around her, it occurs to me that I can learn much from her.

When I started to write this essay, I felt resistance. I use Anishinaabemowin in my work as a way to reclaim my culture, for just as Cedar is rooted in the earth, so my culture is rooted in the language. Surely someone who speaks fluent Anishinaabemowin would be more of an expert on the responsibilities of translating it. After observing how Cedar bows and bends to the wind, I realized my misunderstandings.

They say the language you speak shapes your thoughts, and so it does. Yet, though I only speak English, I do not think in English;

rather, I think in metaphor, allegory, story ... the language of the land. In other words, I think in Anishinaabemowin with English words. Perhaps this is why I became a poet. Because words, sentences, and conversations that fulfill others leave me half heard and wanting. Because I am in a constant state of translation.

Translation is not the moving of words from one language to another, but the process by which we transfer meaning across distance, an act that all writers do. Giizhik has shown me how this essay is the wind, and the ways I must bow and bend with it.

The Truth in Translation
To live truth is to speak only to the extent we have lived or experienced.

My truth is I only speak English. I started translating my work for two main reasons: first, as an act of reclamation to deepen my connection to culture by learning my mother tongue, and second, as a call of accountability for what has been lost within my family and thus my work. As such, I only ever translate my own work, and when I translate it, I am first translating Anishinaabemowin thoughts into poems made of English words, sentences, and phrases; then, second, I am translating selected English words, sentences, and phrases back into Anishinaabemowin. If something is always lost in translation, then much is lost in this process. The interplay between English and Anishinaabemowin is deeply important—how I use a word and where I place it changes its truth.

The Humility of Translation
Be humble, for you walk with yourself to the way you walk
with someone. Think less of oneself in relation to all that sustains us
(plants, animals, minerals, land, water...).

I cannot speak for my culture, for I am only one being within it. I can only speak from within my truth in relation to my place within my culture. Whenever I am translating, I must remember this. I must stay humble in the knowledge of others, who know more about the language, and thus culture, than I.

In my own humility I am reminded of a time when an elder came to visit. He spoke of the importance of Anishinaabe ways of knowing the world—how nothing can be removed from its context, its history, or its language. Another member of my community added to this by saying they think this is where the problem with translation lies. How do you take a language that is process-based, with animate and inanimate beings in relation to one another, and make sense of it within a language that is noun-based and has subjects imposing actions upon agentless objects?

When I translate in my work, I must carry this knowing. Choose words or phrases that have space for the context, history, and language I am moving over distance.

The Respect of Translation
Place others before yourself in your life and don't look down on anyone.
Go easy on one another; on all of creation.

When I choose to translate a word into Anishinaabemowin, it layers my work, as my identity is layered, in relation to others, and this comes with a great responsibility. Ultimately, replacing an English word with Anishinaabemowin is a political act in the sense that it allows access to parts of the story to only a select few. It forces non-Anishinaabemowin speakers to experience the humility of not understanding something and gives Anishinaabemowin speakers the privilege of being the only ones who know; it must be done with great care.

I have a responsibility to choose what I translate with mindfulness; to know who I am translating for; what I am prioritizing in the act of translating. For example, choosing words that only native speakers have access to is deeply different than choosing words that are easily found in the Ojibwe People's Dictionary. The latter means I am translating inclusively, for everyone; however, it also means the nuances of meaning are lost for non-Anishinaabemowin speakers, who rely on the dictionary to understand what is being said.

If you ask the Ojibwe People's Dictionary what the word is for blueberry pie, it will tell you *miini-baashkiminasigani-biitoosijigani-bakwezhigan*. When you break this down, word for word, it will say *miin* is blueberry, *baashkiminasigan* is a sauce or jam, *biitoosijigan* is a pie, and *bakwezhigan* is bannock. This is a very settler understanding of translation: one word for one word. Those who rely on this dictionary to translate my translations for them will lose the context and history of the translation and be left only with the language.

If you ask John Borrows how to say blueberry pie, he will say it is *miini-baashkiminasigani-biitoosijigani-bakwezhigan*. When he translates it, he will tell you it means those new ones waving sticks (after the Baptists) gathering blueberries, placing them between bread, bending over, putting them in the oven, and watching the berries explode. This is a very Anishinaabe knowing of translation: the story in relation to the beings that are being talked about. Those who speak the language within community will have the context, history, and language of what is being said.

I must respect this difference when translating—carefully choose when the nuance of history and context can be lost.

The Love of Translation
Unconditional love between one another, meaning all of creation,
seen and unseen, of yesterday, today, and tomorrow.

My grandmother's mother tongue was forcibly removed by history. When I translate my poetry, I reclaim a voice that misses my tongue. A voice my mother was not allowed to carry.

Choosing to reclaim my great-grandmother's language in my work is a great act of love. Each time I translate my work, I heal the wounds of my heritage, accept my grandmother's choices, send her voice back to her...give her story truth and place it did not receive while she was alive...gift my grandchildren their roots.

The Generosity of Translation
You have the ability to give things away and distribute
what you have. To live correctly and with virtue.

I was taught that all we are is love spiralling into the world. That when we build ourselves in our mothers, first we create our hearts; that we grow ourselves outward from this place where our fire meets water.

If the culture is embedded in the language, then Anishinaabe-mowin is the language of love, and the act of translating what I understand is the giving of love. It is generous in this way.

However, the act of translating is not isolated in a moment. It is organic, in motion, alive in many moments. It can be a hard choice as a poet who writes in two tongues—how much to give and when. Do I include English footnotes in my submissions? Do I translate for an audience when I am giving readings? Are there poems I can't translate? Poems that live in what gets lost? Do I have the ability to give this gift at this time?

I am reminded of a teaching about responsibility and charity. If I come across a man with no fish when I have two, it is my responsibility to give that man one fish, for we both will eat. If I come across a man with no fish when I have two, and I give him both my fish, only one of us will eat and I will expect my community to feed me.

I have also heard this grandfather referred to as honesty, which makes sense to me, for there is great generosity in honesty. It is honest and wise to be responsible; it is dishonest and foolish to be charitable.

And so perhaps the generosity in translating is found by being honest with the work. Who is it for? What is most needed by the poem at that time? Who will grow or benefit from the giving of the translation? Am I giving both fish or only one?

The Courage of Translation
To live with courage is to live with a solid heart. To hold firm
in your thoughts and stand strong, even when you don't
know what will happen right now.

Translation requires great courage, both in the settler-knowing of the word—to feel fear and do what must be done despite it—and in the Anishinaabe-knowing of the word—to live embodied in a good way, with a good heart and good thoughts in one's mind.

To have this courage, I must know myself, listen to my ancestors when they speak within my body, and place trust in all my relations (settler and Indigenous alike). I must clearly see where I am standing in my heart.

My grandmother died with all our names tucked under her tongue. I am a white-coded, non-status, self-identified mixed Indigenous woman speaking about language and culture with my writing. I am hyper-aware that the validity of my Indigenous identity may be called into question every time I publish. If I stand in my heart from the fear of this, then I am imposing my own voice upon my culture when I translate; if I stand in my heart from the responsibility to this, then I follow my teachings, walk with humility, and thus place my voice in relation to others' voices when I translate.

The Wisdom of Translation
Wisdom allows me to eloquently and correctly
interoperate others' ideas. To live with vision.

Again—Anishinaabe culture is embedded in the language—so much is lost in translation. How do you reconcile the way a simple word-for-word translation can still be vastly misunderstood, ill-aligned? Take the word *teaching* as an example. In Anishinaabeg culture, teachings like the Seven Grandfathers would be given to a child in everything they did, so much so that by the age of five or six they would no longer be teachings, rather ways of knowing and relating to the world—aspects of one's being so deeply rooted they would not need to be taught anymore. They would be wisdom carried in the body.

So if there is wisdom in a translation, it is found in the translator's vision, their ability to eloquently and correctly move the distance between two ways of knowing. And just as Giizhik bends and bows to the wind, so I must move my translation to situation. Just as she stands deeply rooted in the earth reaching toward sky, so I must translate while rooted in my culture—responsibly reaching for meaning across distance.

Jagtar Kaur Atwal

FINDING MY VOICE

As a kid I dreamt of being a world-famous author. I remember at fourteen years old sitting in my bedroom, the table pushed against the window, overlooking the row of gardens. Our backyard in the Midlands, England, was plain—grass and weeds and two rusted metal poles, a washing line connecting the posts along the length of the garden. I'd watch Mum hang up the bed-sheets, blankets, Dad's shirts, salwar kameez, and school uniforms, pinning the fabric to the washing line with old wooden pegs. The wet clothes flapped with the breeze like flags. On the warm days, when the washing line was free, my sisters and I would play bad-minton. We'd fight over the green racket, the only one with all the strings.

At fourteen years old I wrote my first story on an old lime-coloured typewriter. I'd push down hard on the black round key tops and watch the thin silver arm strike the black-and-red ribbon, and, with the right amount of pressure, the words would appear on the white paper. I spent most of my time looking for the right letter and other times I'd try to be careful so my finger wouldn't slip in between the gaps of the keys and be mauled by the metal edges.

Language has been a challenge for me; I didn't learn to speak until I was four years old. I attended a special school—not the one for the gifted, but one for those like me who needed help in spoken and written English. I have vague memories, at the age of six, wearing a pink coat with white fur around the hood, clinging to the metal fence, and playing with the other East Indian kids. At eleven, I managed to learn the different letters, and in my mid-twenties, I was able to recite the alphabet in order. I never managed to grasp the phonemic of the alphabet; I couldn't distinguish the different sounds. I have relied on visual memory for the correct letters and sequence to recognize and guess words depending on the context. I skipped the words I couldn't pronounce.

My English assignments would have slashes of red on every line: like pints of blood had been splattered on the pages. It hurt to see the red marks. It was as if someone had punched their hand through my chest and squeezed my heart like a stress ball. How could I be a writer if I couldn't pass English? I tried not to think of having a writer's life. I believed I didn't have the right to it because I couldn't master the dos and don'ts of the language, but still I felt the loss as if I was grieving for someone I never knew.

I have books on the English language with different font sizes, believing that the bigger the font, the better the chance I'll understand. I have books with pictures and with different layouts. I have thick, heavy books and small hand-sized books.

Reading makes me feel as if I'm drowning in a sea of moving words. I concentrate so hard and by the time I've finished a paragraph, I don't always understand what I've read. I'm a visual person and if I can't find a picture for the word, I float over it. I don't remember reading *Snow White*, *Cinderella*, *Little Red Riding Hood*, *Hansel and Gretel*, *Rapunzel*, or even *Goldilocks and the Three Bears*, but I'd flip through the pages and my eyes would stray from the words to the bright blue skies, perfect painted grass, soft lines of white faces, ugly witches with warts the size of chickpeas, and dark skies that winked in the night.

For thirty years I haven't been able to let go of the dream. It's been like a ghost haunting my mind. To exorcise it, I had to register for a writing course. The classroom with rows of tables and chairs reminded me of my own struggles and failures. At high school, I left my final year with seven failed grades and one pass in drama. Every day after the exams, I'd wait for the results. I wanted to get to the school letter before my parents. I'd hear the letterbox snap closed and I'd run to the pile of letters on the carpet at the bottom of the door and quickly flip through them. One morning, mail had arrived for me. I ran up the thirteen steps to my bedroom and leaned against the locked door. I stroked the white paper up to the perforated edge. It felt like silk beneath my thumb. I stopped breathing when I saw the results. I slid down onto the carpet, leaned my head against the door, and started to cry. The following day I lied and told my family I had passed my exams.

I would turn up for the writing class and sit in the same seat at the end of the row. I'd shuffle my unorganized notes into a pile, flip open my brown leather notebook filled with unreadable notes and idle drawings of squares, circles, and lines. I wanted to look the part of a writer. As each class started, my heart would pound against my chest as if it were trying to escape from the room.

Writing has been like trying to walk in knee-deep mud, each step a battle, not just because I've been trying to find the words to tell my story, but the battle to overcome my fear of being rejected by readers because I can't put the comma or the full stop in the right place, or use *their, there,* or *they're* correctly or remember the difference between *choice* and *choose.*

My writer's voice at its rawest and purest is littered with spelling mistakes, missing words, incorrect word usage, poor punctuation and sentence structure. Beneath my errors is a story. I still continue to write even with the thought of rejection because I found another kind of voice—a silenced one.

I REMEMBER AT eleven years old walking home from school alone, dressed in my green jacket and skirt, white shirt, and a matching spiral-coloured tie, carrying my favourite bag. Mum had sewn the bag especially for me. It had yellow, red, and orange flowers and large green leaves. On the bottom was a big ink mark: I had left the top loose on a felt-tip blue pen.

My right hand trailed the six-foot-high wall made of large red bricks. My fingertips travelled along the bumps and dents of the bricks as if I was reading Braille. I followed the curve onto the street I lived on. My home was forty-four doors away. Two white boys were heading toward me, one built like a quarterback, his cheeks pink, and the other a skinny pole. The quarterback spat at me and his spittle landed on my lapel. I felt the hardness of the wall against my back as I tried to push into it. The quarterback said, "Get out of our country." The skinny boy repeatedly dropped his soccer ball hard on the concrete slabs before it bounced back into his hands. Bang. Bang. Bang. I kept my eyes on the fractured slab I stood on. I held my breath until I felt as if my lungs were burning. I didn't have any words as the clear spit soaked into the green lapel. Their voices became a whisper as they disappeared around the curve. I ran home and hid in my bedroom.

Soon after that, I stopped wearing salwar kameez suits outside the house so the bright colours wouldn't get me noticed. I wished I could change my colour and be white like the other kids at school and fit in with my neighbours. Mrs. Greenberg on the right side, with perfectly cut grass, not a bald or brown patch in sight, and Miss Lane on the left, whose wall I'd climb to fetch the white plastic shuttlecock shaped like a rocket hidden beneath the big rhubarb leaves.

I wrote my first story about two white kids, a brother and sister who were visiting their grandparents at their cottage and became mixed up in an old robbery and raced to discover the stolen buried money. I'd got my ideas from my favourite TV shows. I'd sit cross-legged on the paisley-patterned carpet in the living room, just two feet away from the television, watching *Magnum P.I.*, *Charlie's Angels*, *Mac-Gyver*, *Wonder Woman*, and *Knight Rider* that played on the thirty-six-inch screen with a dial knob. The shows would swallow me up. When the credits rolled, my insides shrivelled up like a dried prune because I knew I was the wrong colour. In my stories I'd travel the world, arrest villains, fly planes, speed on the highway as I weaved in between the cars, and I would become a white girl from the Midlands.

AT NINE YEARS OLD, my sisters and I spent Wednesday evenings at the local Gurdwara on Stanhope Road to study Punjabi. Two Victorian houses converted into our local temple. We studied in a large room; there were no tables or chairs. The room was always cold. I'd sit on the red rug with my legs stretched out in front and my jacket wrapped around me to keep the heat in, my notepad balanced on my thighs. I'd copy the letters the teacher wrote on the blackboard. He never smiled and I never remembered him blinking, just staring, daring us to give him the wrong answer. He wore a turban and had a long, straggly black beard. He'd use the long, thick wooden stick to smack each letter on the board. I would chew on my yellow pencil. As everyone recited the letters, they sounded like an out-of-tune choir. I'm not fluent in Punjabi, my second language. Of the thirty-five consonants and vowels, I never got past the first five letters.

My sisters and I knew we'd have an arranged marriage after we settled in a job because it's part of our Sikh culture. I learned to clean and cook so I could be a good wife one day. Mum would be in the kitchen; the aroma of chicken cubes sizzling in onions and ghee would drift into the corridor while we carried out our chores. The noise of the vacuum would keep my mum at bay. I'd drag the Hoover handle along the same spot, my eyes glued to the television. When it was my turn to do the bathroom, I'd run the tap, the water splashing around the porcelain sink as I leaned out of the window and watched the white kids play outside.

I knew I didn't want to get married but I also knew there were only so many times I could say no before my parents made the decision. I didn't have the words in Punjabi or English or the courage to tell them I was gay.

Mrs. Strafford was everyone's favourite teacher, but she was my first crush. I sat on the end of the long table and scribbled in my schoolbook as she walked from one end of her desk to the other, her hands flying in the air as she talked, holding a piece of chalk as if it were a cigarette. I'd watch her every move, and when Mrs. Stafford walked by my desk and gently tapped my shoulder, my skin tingled with excitement. At thirteen, I knew it was wrong because girls had boyfriends and boys had girlfriends.

I used to dream that one day I would just tell Mum and Dad what I was going through and they would give me a hug and tell me everything was going to be okay. I knew I was only fooling myself. In reality, I was frightened of what they would do if they knew. They might have thrown my clothes in a suitcase, made phone calls, and sent me to India to be married, and I wouldn't be able to fight back.

In 2005, after years of silence, before I left England to start fresh in Toronto, I decided to tell my sister I was gay. I remember my finger shook as I pressed hard at the numbers on the keypad, each breath shorter and quicker as I waited.

"Hello."

"Hi, it's me. I called to tell you something," I said.

"What is it?"

"Promise you won't tell Mum and Dad or anyone?"

"I won't," she said with a wobble in her voice.

"You know why I won't get married?"

"Is it because you like a guy Mum and Dad won't like?"

"I'm gay," I said quickly.

"I know this divorced guy, no children."

"Did you hear what I said?"

"You can meet him on your own terms."

MAY 2015, I SAT ACROSS from the white screen, my back curved into the wooden spindles of a chair. I twisted my neck a touch to the right and looked out the small rectangular window, streaks of white clouds slicing through the blue morning sky. I listened to the chatter of the birds hidden in the overgrown ivy while the cursor blinked. I had written a dozen short stories, but it was Cheryl Strayed's *Wild* that encouraged me to step into my writing as a gay Sikh woman. In *Tiny Beautiful Things* it was as if she was giving me permission to share my life.

I could feel my body pulling away, the space dense beneath my fingers as they hovered over the keys. I closed my eyes to hold back the tears, not because I couldn't find words but at what I was feeling when I looked back at my life. I wanted to scream until my throat dried up. I covered my face with my hands as I tried to hold back the loud sobs. I wiped my nose, leaving a wet dark stripe along the red sleeve. My skin stung. I wanted to get a baseball bat and smash the computer over and over and over and swing, swing, and swing at the pictures of Mum and Dad. Swing the wooden bat at books on the shelves, until everything was broken, like me.

WORKING THROUGH THE drafts of this essay has helped me acknowledge that I process things slower and my struggle with words doesn't mean my brain has rejected the written language. It is simply wired differently. I hoped writers and readers would accept my faulty writer's voice, but it turned out the only person who needed to accept it was me.

At fourteen, I wrote to escape my life and live in a world of make-believe, a place I could control, where I could be anyone. Creative non-fiction has taken me on a journey I never expected. At the beginning, the drive was to see my name in print and have a chance to call myself a writer, but when I stepped into my writing, I discovered sharing my life on paper had become a tool to mend my silent past and explore who I am. *Gay* is still the hardest word to type. When I see the letters on the screen, I duck down behind the computer and look over my shoulder, wondering how my family would react if they read my work.

My stories are hard to get out. It's like trying to open up a tin of chunky chicken soup with a flat Phillips screwdriver because, for the first time in my life, I'm using my voice.

TÉA MUTONJI

COMFORT LANGUAGE

1.

After immigrating to Canada, Yoni and I were thrown into English schools, which, to my memory, is my first moment of disorientation. We sat on the curb at recess, watching life unfold, getting a feel of this new land, sticking out our tongues to taste the air, here. I felt mute, filled with this awareness that the life I knew was gone. My body, my space, my tender-as-a-dandelion brother were all unrecognizable to me. But I wouldn't say that immigrating was hard. It just took something from us that is impossible to replace. There was a van and then there was a car and then there was a plane and then there were the falls in St. Catherines. If I knew then how to speak the language of my Canadian family, I would have said, "The earth is cleansing." That's just the sort of kid I was, observant and romantic. Instead, I reached for the falls and remained in awe. Suddenly I was speechless. There is a certain loss of self that comes with the loss of language. I didn't know then that I would spend the next twenty years unlearning how to silence myself, searching for the right words. I watched the colours the water could make and wondered how it could slip in and out of reds. I was six, Yoni was nine, so naturally, in the blink of an eye, we were fluent. Still, that feeling I had on that curb revisits me after a break-up, when I fail an assignment, and when I lose my wallet. All these unrelated histories remind me that once I stood on the quiet earth, holding on to my brother's pinky, not sure of the word for *fingers*.

2.

Both my parents went to school, and my siblings and I watched *Inuyasha*. We would rock-paper-scissors and sometimes watch *Beyblade* instead. *Sailor Moon* was reserved for the weekends. Animes were especially good because the characters used their bodies to speak. If you paid close attention to the subtitles and the way Kagome's face fumbled, you would know that the words on the screen meant: *Stay with me*. Before bed, my mother would tell me about her early evenings at the ESL centre, about the woman who reminds her of one of her sisters, about the long bus rides through Scarborough, how the world goes from green to yellow and the occasional fireworks in daylight. Soon my mother will graduate college, get a full-time nursing job at a long-care facility, and become nostalgic about the smell of back home, the hospital floors where she once worked. Our pre-prayer night routine will be replaced by her homework. She'll sit at the foot of my bed, and I'll listen to the stories about her patients, and I'll write them down on her charts and incident reports. She'd ask me, how do you say *this* in English, like a game of charades, showing me where a patient complained of pain.

3.

In Kinshasa, I used to recite poems and stories, mostly in French and sometimes in Lingala. They were folktales that had been passed down from generations of Congolese women. I would recite them at churches, at talent shows, in the middle of the street. My favourite was "Femme African," a poem or a mantra that began with: "Femme Noirs, Femme African, quant je te regards, des larmes coules de mes yeux." And that's it. That's all I remember. Sometimes I feel the guilt of being the last carrier of this offering, having been too preoccupied between integration and childhood to keep it somewhere safe. It was no surprise to anyone that a few years into our cultural assimilation, I found myself onstage again. I was committed to my acting career. Through an art program for underprivileged youths, I worked closely with a theatre instructor who encouraged me to lose my accent. This was done with a generous amount of lyrics by Fefe Dobson and Avril Lavigne, until I too sounded like a perfect Canadian. In the casting room, while my fellow actors practised their lines with the guardians, I helped my mother with her medical documents. I could tell she was struggling, the way her turtle body closed into her shaking hands.

4.

In Scarborough, languages were traded like Valentine Grams. Across the roundabout, the family from the West Indies spoke with plates of roti at the neighbourhood cookout; the one from Haiti said bonjour by dropping the *r*, a half-French so intimate to us, hearing it still gives me goosebumps. The little Cuban boy argued that he wasn't Black, but no matter how you spin it, the word for *nigger* is nigger. It felt good being here. It felt like home. And then in the spring of 2008, my family packed our bags and we headed out east, where there was a field of grass and the heavy smell of farm animals.

High school happened. It was what it was. Complicated. Shuffling through the politics of Franco-Ontarians, who spoke a French different than ours. I was always reminded that my French was borrowed or a life sentence. How colonizers planned to keep their hold on our people in such a subtle way, we're only now noticing it.

In my third year of university, I changed my major from political science to English. If I couldn't change the world, perhaps I could get the tools to help me make sense of it. My parents called to share their concerns, but I ignored them to avoid hearing the voice of parents who wished to make lawyers out of their children. At twenty, after I got promoted at the pub, I printed out a diploma that said I'd passed the bar. The joke fell flat on its face when I had to explain that I've become a *bar*-tender. We didn't speak for a few years after that for unrelated matters. Later, through a sibling, my mother got in touch with the news of my father's diagnosis. I reckon that when she said, Je ne comprends pas, she meant, *I need you.* I began attending doctor visits with my parents as their translator.

Coming back home, I was pleased to see that my parents had made a life for themselves. Up until that point, I only knew them as people who worked very hard to catch up with this new country. Five, ten, fifteen years in Canada, it was obvious that this home would never be theirs. Now they cleaned and danced on Sundays. They shopped at the same grocery store, they watched sitcoms like *Black-ish* and *Modern Family.* Several nights a week my mother made Canadian mac and cheese, calling it the most complicated recipe to follow.

5.

When I was writing my first book, I often called my mother to ask, "How do you say this in Lingala?" or, "What's the Swahili word for that?" leaping at this second chance to be her daughter. Every so often, my mother gave me a piece of my childhood back. She'd tell me about that time at our citizenship ceremony, how I insisted on singing the national anthem in English and in French. I asked if she'd made any friends at work. This was around her tenth-year anniversary at the nursing home. She told me the tension was a matter of politics and language. "We don't understand each other, culture is so different, we don't communicate well." I called her again after I got broken up with. I let her pray for my healing. She sang in French but praised in Tshiluba, while I wept quietly in English.

I joke that the freedom in my writing is that my parents never read it. I say, it's not that they can't, it's that they don't have the patience for the language. As an exercise, I translated one of my stories for my mother. About a week later, we found out that the French rights to my collection had been bought by a Montreal publisher. Once, at a book award, Kathleen Newman-Bremang walked up to my mother and told her she thought I was wonderful. My mother was excited to be there, to be recognized, to be approached by another Black woman. Later, when she retold this story, she said, "You're my Canadian Idol."

While on my book tour, I took my mother across the country. On our way, a rare six days of closeness ahead, my mother's eyes widened every time I ordered something over five dollars—a Starbucks coffee, a gluten-free vegan muffin, and then a wine on the plane. It was the wine that tipped her over the edge. I knew I was in trouble whenever she'd switch to French. "My fille," she told me, "is this how you waste your money?" I realized she probably wanted a glass too but didn't know how to ask. I was twenty-five and my mother was fifty-seven. All the mother-daughter spending times we've shared before my recent career have been survival activities: grocery shopping, doctor visits, hair-combing sessions. I was thinking about this while we were at a seafood restaurant in Vancouver. It sat on a shore, the goddamn sun glistening. We took turns posing for photographs. This was the first time my mother and I were at dinner together, just the two of us.

My mother asked me to order her a salad and I did. She paid attention to her surroundings. It wasn't until we were ordering our mains that I noticed that my mother was struggling to read the menu. At first she said she didn't have her reading glasses, but then she ordered a meal with bacon, to which I said, "But you don't eat pork," to which she responded, "Je ne comprends pas." I gave her a menu tour. I'm used to romanticizing a meal. Whenever I trained new staff, I called this stage storytelling. What does this meal say about this particular guest? What does this drink say about the night to come? This meal said that my mother who works in English and uses it every day, colloquially, cannot process unfamiliar words. Like *charcuterie*, like *peppercorn*. Our meals arrived and we ate in silence.

6.

After our Vancouver trip, I spent a few months living with my parents during a global pandemic. While I was writing, my father called me to the living room so I could order the next season of *Black-ish* on YouTube. I showed him how to do it for next time. A week later, once my parents had burned through every episode of their latest season, my father called again.

After dinner, the three of us sat in the living room. I watched as my father paused to translate for my mother. "Tu comprends?" he'd ask before unpacking the joke. When he fell asleep, my mother revealed to me that he needs to feel important. It helps with his seizures, she said, it's good to let him feel needed.

7.

During my short stay, my father and I fought once a week. He is soft and uses poetry as a form of expression. I am private and use poetry as a means to an end. In a screaming match, I find his speech too riddled with metaphor. In contrast, I am curt and uninterested in the theatrics. I finished a call in the formal dining room where I had a better reception and heard my parents talking about me in Tshiluba. My father argued that the world has made me cold. My mother rebutted that English is just a bleak language. The teen girl in me couldn't help but reveal herself. I was hot and suddenly seventeen again. To my father I said, "Do you want to say that to my face?" and he looked at me like I was unrecognizable.

My teen room felt cold and empty, and my thoughts bounced off the walls like acoustic whispers. In French, I would have said, "Veux tu bien m'adresser?" which is polite. Which asks, would you "love" to speak with me? Knowing my father, he would have said, "Yes, I would very much love to speak to you!" We couldn't agree on language, so I packed my bags and retreated to my apartment downtown.

A week later he sent me a text, which was half poem, half apology. I Google-translated most of it, ready to confront this part of myself I'd lost. I mourned by writing several poems about our summer trip to Belgium in 2008, the summer I turned fourteen. My Euro auntie had corrected me whenever I said, "Comment allez-vous?" instead of "Comment va tu?" She said the latter means we are intimate, while the former means we are meeting for the first time. I walked around my apartment studying my father's text. Full of desperation, passion, vulnerability, and pain. The long prose reminded me of a message I had sent a previous lover shortly after our relationship was over. I concluded that he is a philosopher, I am a poet, we use language differently. And it suddenly dawned on me: Dad and I are one and the same.

8.

I went about with the new life I had made for myself, in my apartment, in my career, and found myself constantly worried about my parents. Their safety, their future, the way in which they interacted with the world. The effects of old age, the dementia neither one of them shows signs of having but, hey, anything is possible. My mother texted and asked me to order her a meal from UberEats because she doesn't know how. My father FaceTimed to ask where to get cashmere sweaters, and when I told him everywhere, he texted back all in caps, OU!?!? I felt happy to have this relationship with my parents and yet burdened by this closeness. For once, I cared for myself and only myself. A special kind of luxury most big families, immigrant children, don't get. I wanted to milk it while I still could. Go back to that limbo period in which my parents didn't need me and my siblings didn't need me and even I didn't need me. I don't know if it's selfish but mostly I felt scared and somewhat angry that while I learned the language, the ways, the ideology, the beliefs of this new world, my parents were merely getting by.

9.

On my next visit, I sat my parents down and asked if they would consider moving to Ottawa. In my mind, this was a compromise. A way for me to live my life and worry less about the ways in which they would live theirs. I said, "What if you need to call a taxi to the hospital? Let me hear it, what would you say?" Neither one of them plan to retire in the next ten years (which, frankly, is stressful, considering my father's epilepsy). I heard myself say: "I need you to live in a city where you'll need me less."

The conversation was halted. We will talk about it when it will be time. But that's exactly what I'm afraid of. My parents and how unseriously they feel about time. How "in time," my mother will be very good at English, and how "in time," my father will shop by himself. I realized that sometimes when I looked at my parents, I saw my brother and me on that curb at recess, stuck in a time warp.

10.

I know little about how to negotiate time. In the same way I know little about how to weave my way in and out of language. This seems bizarre because I'm a writer and interact with language as my daily practice, but every new day I am learning that language is not just about words. Very little of it is about the things we say. It has more to do with the things we understand. In French, the direct translation insists that we say, "I lack you," when we mean, "I wish you were here." I try to remember that. To use it as my operational definition. To understand that there is a difference between being "loved" and being "loving." Language has a way to reveal oneself, less about getting to where we are going and more about hanging on. So I FaceTime both my parents via group chat. My father picks up from the living room, my mother from the kitchen. I am sitting at my desk in my apartment. They tell me about their day, their latest Netflix binge, each of us speaking in our comfort language.

Rowan McCandless

WHAT ARE YOU?
A FIELD STUDY

*Until the lion learns how to speak, all stories will glorify
the hunter.*

—AFRICAN PROVERB

A Typical Exchange

Setting: A physician's office at a walk-in clinic.
Physician: If you don't mind my asking, what are you?
Me: I'm Canadian.
Physician: No really, what are you?
Me: I'm eighth-generation Canadian on one side of
my family and third-generation on the other.
Doctor: Seriously, what are you? Where are your
people from?*
Me: My father is *Black,* and my mother is *white.*
Doctor: I knew there was something about you.
[end of exchange]

* What are you? Where are your people from? Translation: *I'm uncom-fortable in your presence and don't know how I am supposed to engage with you because I can't tell your ethnicity. But if I have an idea where your ancestors come from, I would know what category to put you in.*

1. Questions and Thoughts on What are you?

For most of my life as a racialized woman, I've struggled to find ade-quate words to respond to the question "What are you?" I found the English language profoundly self-limiting. There was no way for me to respond, given my belief that the question itself implied the accep-tance of race and racial divides, of being othered, and of taking on the discomfort of the person asking the question at my expense.

I've often wondered how I could express myself when the ques-tion itself was reductionist. How could I express myself, after being linguistically tongue-tied by Euro-colonialism? How could I express myself when there were so many native languages now lost to me?

2. Glossary

- **Africadian:** A term that closely resonated with me, coined by George Elliott Clarke. Africadian—someone who is a descendant of the distinct cultural communities formed by Black Canadians in Nova Scotia and New Brunswick. Africadian was a word that spoke to me of home, of my paternal line of grandmothers, cous-ins, and aunties; of my grandmother's ancestors who came from Nova Scotia. It spoke of a link to the past, to a distinct dialect I rec-ognized upon hearing, and to a sense of identity and belonging.
- **Bi-racial:** A racial term used to describe a person born to parents of two different ethnic backgrounds. More commonly used for individuals having one Black and one white parent. Bi-racial was a word that caused me grief growing up. It made me feel like I didn't really belong to either of my parents; that I was somehow destined to live a hyphenated existence. That hyphen cast a long

shadow, one near impossible to escape from. It offered a life lived in liminal spaces, the linguistically in-between.

- **Black:** A racial term used to describe the descendants of the transatlantic slave trade. After being called coloured during my childhood, at the age of twelve I was told by my mother that if anyone asked, I was to tell them I was Black. I wondered if my mother ever considered how rejected this made me feel: the denial of maternal blood ties. As for my father, he never commented that often on race and was more concerned with my appearance and academic achievements.

- **Coloured:** A racial term, dated, used to define people with black or brown skin. My paternal grandmother, Daisy, used the word coloured to describe herself, as well as family and community members. Myself, I hated being called coloured as a child. It made me feel like my personhood was less than and as insignificant as a crayon colour. I thought if white and peach were colours in the crayon box, then why was I the only one who qualified as coloured?

- **Diaspora:** According to the *Merriam-Webster* dictionary, the word diaspora is derived from the Greek word diaspeirein, meaning to scatter, spread about. Diaspora—the migration of a population from their homelands. I have considered saying that I am the daughter of multiple diasporas, the descendants of enslaved people, European serfs, and British Empire Loyalists. That on my mother's side I was Polish and either Scottish, Irish, or British. While on my father's side I was Africadian and African American, in addition to _____, _____, and _____.* But then the thought arises "Why should I?" Why should I have to explain my ethnic background to someone who was asking the question from a position of power, an entrenched sense of belonging, and systemic white privilege.

- **Gullah:** At times, I'm saddened that I do not carry the South Carolinian lilt of my paternal grandfather. Lost was the unique language that evolved along South Carolina's coast and nearby islands—Gullah, a mixture of African languages that merged with English during the transatlantic slave trade. Nor am I aware of the languages excised from ancestral memory—the language of enslaved people from Africa, possibly Yoruba, Igbo, or Hausa—thanks to English, the language of empire and oppression. English, an insidious language of a majority that had supplanted and eradicated my inheritance of numerous native tongues. English, a language used as a weapon of indoctrination. English, a language of cultural assimilation, one that shamed my great-grandparents for speaking Polish. English, a language of cultural genocide, leading to the complete erasure of the languages spoken by enslaved people from Africa. I understand that my tongue has been colonized. No linguistic muscle memory of home exists.

- **Heinz 57:** A racial term used to describe someone of multiple ethnicities. A phrase I tried to make use of lightheartedly as a teenager to describe myself when asked the question "What are you?"

- **Mulatto:** A racial term derived from the Portuguese and Spanish mulato, derived from the Portuguese mula from the Latin mūlus meaning mule—the infertile hybrid offspring of a horse and a donkey. Mulatto, a racial term used to describe a person who has one Black and one white parent. I was called mulatto in junior high school. Not knowing what the word meant, I looked it up in the dictionary. The definition made me feel like I was somehow unnatural. A mistake created by a mistake.

- **Mutt:** A racial term used to describe a person who has an ethnically diverse background. Derogatory, lesser than when compared to the value placed on purebreds.

- **Negro:** A racial term, dated, now considered offensive by many people: used to describe those who are native to or descended from Africa and classified according to physical features (such as dark skin pigmentation).

- **Nigger:** A racial slur, derogatory, used against Black people. The word descends from the Spanish word negro, a derivative of the Latin word niger, meaning black.
- **Object:** A thing. Object. Objects. Objectified. I have always carried the pain of wanting to articulate who I was as a human being as opposed to being perceived as an object and being objectified. For people to recognize that I was: mother, friend, teacher, student, writer, daughter, sister, niece, cousin, auntie, lover, wife, ex. Language as relational rather than confrontational.
- **Passing:** My mother insisted that I identify as Black. And maybe I was in some circles. But in others I was called coloured, negro, nigger, mulatto, mixed, mutt, half-breed, Heinz 57, Oreo, half-and-half, my complexion too dark for some and too light for others. *Stay out of the sun. Stop acting white. You're lucky; you can pass.* "Pass for what?" I often felt like saying but didn't.
- **Polish:** On my maternal side, my Polish ancestry can be traced to a tiny village called Ruda Różaniecka. Ruda: Polish (fem) meaning "ore." Różaniecka: Polish (fem) różaniec: meaning "rosary." Ruda Różaniecka, a word I can transcribe but only mispronounce.
- **Unilingual:** Using one language exclusively. I have considered the impact of being unilingual when it comes to self-definition and determination. What it means to only speak English, the language of historical, colonial, and intergenerational oppression. For me, the English language is one of loss: lost stories, lost world views, lost customs, and lost connections to the past. I carry inside of me the impact, the pain of coming from so many linguistic backgrounds—all shorn from my tongue.
- **White:** A racial term used to describe those of European ancestry who are classified according to physical features (such as light skin pigmentation).

* Please note, family secrets impacted my access to crucial information. I knew that my maternal great-grandfather ran out on his family, leaving a wife and two young daughters behind. I remember that his last name was Atkinson, but nothing about his origins. On my paternal side, slavery and the rape of my ancestors by slave owners rendered it impossible for me to provide further information of familial ties and languages spoken.

3. Scenes

In April 2020, I signed up for online Polish classes. In the time of Covid, with life shut down, I thought now was the time to pick up the language my mother and maternal side had denied me. Despite my best efforts, by lesson two, I was disheartened. I found the materials difficult to remember and my pronunciation left much to be desired.

On two occasions, I purchased Ancestry DNA test kits for personal use. I ordered the second kit because the first one had spent a year and a half in my sock drawer, and I worried it might have reached its best-before date. So far, I haven't made use of either kit. I'm reluctant to spit into a test tube, mail my sample off, and wait for the results because I question the benefits to be gained. The knowledge would not restore erased cultures back to me, the names of my ancestors, or the ability to think and speak in native tongues that were supplanted by the English language. Although it may have pointed out the ethnic groups to which I belonged, it would not have solved my discomfort when asked, "What are you?"

I wondered why I was the recipient of "the question" in the first place. Why I was left with only the conquerors' tongue to express my experience of being othered. Why I felt guilty putting aside my discomfort for the sake of an overcurious white person asking the question.

4. Field Notes

The English language framed my understanding of the world, provided an outlook on the human experience, identity, and a way of being. It relayed a tale of belonging or of being an outsider. It provided me with scant family history: few answers to who I was or where I came from. Language could bestow continuity between generations, but that was a gift stolen from me. I'm more familiar with English language as a system of erasure, domination, and oppression. Being an English-language speaker made me feel like something was missing from my life: ways of thinking, ways of articulating and understanding the world around me. I mourn the many languages that were taken from me, the possibility of not being viewed as an outsider or defined by the colour of my skin.

I WAS FOUR the first time I heard the word *nigger*. It was in the basement of my paternal grandmother's church. Along with Grandma Daisy, we had just watched a children's play and were getting ready to leave. While my grandmother said her farewells to her fellow congregants, I sat beside a much older boy within a row of empty metal folding chairs. He looked at me with meanness in his eyes and said, "Get away from me, nigger." I didn't know what the word *nigger* meant, but I understood by his tone and the way he was looking at me that it was a word that carried viciousness, a word that belied the children's rhyme "Sticks and stones may break your bones, but names will never hurt you." I never told my grandmother what transpired in that church basement. I was too ashamed, as if there was some part of me that was so vile that it justified such an attack.

I WAS SIX, playing in the front yard of my best friend, Kathy, along with a clutch of local neighbourhood kids. Someone had brought a large rubber ball with them, the kind that stung the skin upon contact. We played a game, one I no longer remember the rules for. I can recall that one player tossed the ball high into the air, while everyone shouted out, *One. Two. Three. Nigger babies*, as Kathy's dad watched from the front stoop. The next thing I remember was my father walking past a half-dozen houses before silently taking my hand and leading me home. That was the day I learned what *that* word meant. That was the day my father sat me down on the living room couch and, with a pained expression, explained to his daughter what *that* word meant. That was the day he informed me that despite going to the same Catholic church, the same Sunday and elementary schools, eating the same foods on special occasions—perogies, cabbage rolls, cabbage buns, and kielbasa—I was not the same as my friends.

THE SUMMER I TURNED twelve, members of the royal family toured Manitoba in celebration of the province's centennial. In Winnipeg, the Prince of Wales and Princess Anne were participating in the opening of a nursing home's newest wing. My family made the pilgrimage to view the festivities. After my father dropped us off, he left to park the car. Along with my brothers, I trailed after our mother as she searched for a spot to watch from the crowd, finally settling on a location next to two elderly women dressed in black, their grey hair covered with babushkas.

I listened as they traded idle pleasantries in Polish with my mother—a language she never taught nor shared with me or my brothers. My ears and brain strained to understand the words being spoken between them, but my nascent vocabulary consisting of the names of food brought out for special occasions or the couple of swear words my maternal grandfather had taught me left me woefully at a disadvantage. I resented my mother, in that moment, because I felt like an outsider to a language that should have been mine by birthright.

When my father showed up, and the two age-bent women realized that my parents were together, their faces soured and they started talking between themselves, turning their backs on my mother. While I couldn't understand what was being spoken, their sideways glances, furrowed brows, and looks of disgust were enough for me to understand that they disapproved of my family.

"Let's go," my mother said, cognizant of every derisive word they had uttered in Polish.

Her anger parted the crowd as we followed in her wake.

AS A TEENAGER and adult, I was called *exotic* by my friends. They spoke the word *exotic* wistfully, as if it bore the weight of romanticized adolescent longing. *Exotic*—the word embarrassed me, made me feel self-conscious about my body, the sexual vibes I worried I was giving off. Because I had no way to push back, the word *exotic* made me wish I was invisible, which caused me to wear layers of clothing to hide my body. Being viewed as exotic meant being viewed through the white male gaze. It meant being fetishized, a characterization that made me extremely uncomfortable, as if my entire existence and self-worth were predicated on being a sexual object.

"WHAT ARE YOU?"

My fallback answer, "My father is Black, and my mother is white," was a statement that made me feel complicit in the acceptance of race as a valid biological system.

"What are you?"

There was no way for me to answer the question without feeling defeated, othered, and split in two.

"What are you?"

There is no way for me to answer the question. Ultimately, I am at a loss for words.

Sahar Golshan

YE KAM

was born on the northeast end of a massive bicontinental island in one of its largest cities. Here in Tkaronto, I am one of six cousins in my maternal family to be born outside of the Asian continent. We make up the first generation who do not speak Teochew fluently. In my father's family, I am the only person who was not born in Iran, the only non-fluent speaker of Farsi.

This entrenched non-proficiency made me a language learner. It gave rise to a lifelong obsession with the accumulation of missing vocabulary.

HAJI AND I first met at Pearson Airport when I was six. I was put into a poofy white dress with peach roses. He landed wearing a dark grey suit. I hadn't been keen on joining for the airport pickup. My perfect school attendance record was on the line. Plus, the timing was horrible. Mahin and Haji were arriving on Chocolate Art Day.

Although I'd never met him, I had spent the first six years of my life listening to stories about Haji and my grandmother Mahin in

Iran. Because my grandparents had been introduced to me in this way, I didn't know how to interact with them as real people. On that first day, I looked to my dad every time my grandfather spoke, needing him to bring Haji to life for me.

For one month our white-walled one-bedroom apartment in downtown Tkaronto became the home of five: my grandparents, my parents, and me. In his teens and early twenties, my father had been involved with an anti-government organization that was outlawed in Iran after the revolution of 1979. Living in Canada in 1996, he feared the repercussions of returning to his home country, given the mercilessness of the prevailing Islamic Republic. For this reason, my paternal grandparents visited us instead of the other way around. My father said that soon things would change. That one day, we too would be allowed to live in Iran. It was my favourite story. The tale of permanent reunion.

My grandfather stood three inches taller than his son. Haji had olive skin and white hair that he was delighted to have his Chinese daughter-in-law dye black. He rarely spoke. Having grown up with two deaf brothers, he communicated mostly with his eyes, face, and hands. This worked well for me as I did not speak Farsi. When Haji did speak, I got to hear his soft and high-pitched voice.

During the visit, my dad got his parents to get their headshots taken, with the hope that the images would serve for their Canadian identification cards. He was homesick and wanted them to leave Iran permanently and come live with us. At the photo studio, Haji wore the same grey suit from the day he landed.

My grandmother Mahin had white skin and short black hair. She stood under five feet tall. In the basement parking lot of our apartment, she loved to challenge me to race her to our car. Often, she would beat me to the red Toyota Corolla.

"Maa-maan, stay here," my father would say.

"Stay? You haven't even bought a house. How can we stay?"

"If you two live here, I won't have a reason to want to go back. We'll finally buy a house. A big house. Please stay." He asked them every day.

My dad wanted my help with his mission. He taught me to say, "Mahin, okay Canada," to my grandmother and, "Haji, okay Canada," to my grandfather.

"Mahin, okay Canada!" I would repeat.

"Nah! Sahar, okay *Iran*!" she would protest.

By the end of the month, I became sick of our guests. Of their food, their clothes, and the flowery queen-size mattress that took up too much space in the living room. I began begging them to go back home. Too young for homework, I spent my afternoons after school demanding they leave.

"I cannot stay here, Mamal, even your daughter wants me go."

My grandparents didn't like Canada. Their visit was in late spring, but they were aware that our winters were extremely cold. They preferred life in central Iran, where an average summer day burns at forty degrees Celsius. Back home, they owned land that produced magnificent fruit and nut trees. Their remaining three children lived in Iran and they were starting families. The two worlds did not compare.

Although the visit had been short, I thought about them every time I entered the classroom. I was the only student without a milk-chocolate painting mounted on the wall.

MY PARENTS' LANGUAGES always hovered around me, though at a distance. Of the two, Teochew felt closer. My maternal grandparents were volunteers at the temple on Cecil Street by the Spadina Chinatown. In the supermarkets, everyone spoke Cantonese. At the temple it was different. All I heard inside was Teochew. Here, knowing my language felt important. When Gong and Ma passed away, it's where we burned incense.

Chinatown was also a special place because it was where my parents met. My father had been a driving instructor in the late eighties. When one of his students finally passed his road test, he treated my dad to dinner at a restaurant on Dundas just east of Spadina. The student brought his girlfriend, who in turn brought her friend to the celebration: my mother.

MY FATHER SAYS my brain knew how to detect different languages from an early age. He says I could tell that my maternal grandmother spoke to me in Teochew and my own mother did too, especially when we were alone. I was aware that my dad spoke Farsi, even if, unlike Teochew, I didn't understand it.

He says I understood Teochew and Farsi were different from the language I heard spoken at daycare and on TV. Although neither of my parents spoke English fluently, the language still held intimate status in our household. Because my parents didn't learn each other's languages, English became our unofficial home language. Born out of necessity. Up until today, it functions as a semi-sticking glue that keeps disparate elements of my family life together.

My greatest attachment to the English language came from reading. I bulldozed through stacks of chapter books about preteen girls and their babysitting enterprise. Though I was an only child, I pretended the brothers and sisters of my favourite characters were my own. Sometimes I lied and told my classmates that my book siblings were real. The concept of a big, united family was fascinating to me, but I found the idea of a twin the most compelling. I dreamt of an identical sister who could understand exactly what it was like to be me.

Deep in the pages, I had exchanges I couldn't have with my parents. Our proximities to English were too mismatched. My father spoke English as a third language. My mother spoke it as a fifth.

"SALAAM SALAAAM! KHUB HASTID?! HASTE NABAASHID. KHASHI?" Our bungalow shook on Saturday mornings. My father spoke in shouts when he called his family in Iran. It was the day of the week when I saw him smile with all his teeth, yellowed by Du Maurier Regular cigarettes. He thought his roaring telephone voice could cut the distance made by decades of regime-sanctioned separation. After chatting with his siblings for five minutes, he would pass me the phone as if I'd made a special request for it. His dark brown eyes bulged out. "Oh! Sahar joon wants to speak with you."

I squinted my face tight and shook my head no. His energy lowered, so I tried to pick it back up with the phone. These were the only Farsi lessons I got. I repeated everything he'd said to my aunt and uncles. Instead I would have liked to ask them, "Do you know who I am? Do you wish you could see me?"

As a child, I viewed the Persian language as someone else's script. To me it was a cryptic work of poetry, not meant for me to understand.

When I turned twenty, I picked up the poem again. I enrolled in an introductory Iranian language course offered at my university. On the first day, I nervously entered the brightly lit classroom and took in the four long, rectangular desks positioned on each side. They faced a larger one at the front by the blackboard. When the teacher entered the room, she asked us to share why we were studying Farsi. I felt as if I was being examined under an X-ray, like I had to share the reason I was missing all the ribs on the right side of my body.

To acknowledge this absence was to acknowledge a part of myself I had not yet learned to accept. I was confessing that I was unfamiliar to myself.

I told my classmates I clammed up when my father passed me the phone to speak to my family in Iran. My goal was to have my first untranslated conversation with my grandparents.

I didn't share with the class the fact that when my dad had been the same age, he had left Iran for good. His political exile from the country where all his family remained meant I had had very little access to Farsi.

Instead of language lessons, he taught me to fear the Islamic Republic of Iran. In lieu of lullabies, he told me stories of imprisoned activists who were tortured by the regime. He recounted tales of prison guards who notoriously sewed up the mouths of prisoners with needles as punishment for speaking out.

Our class met three days a week for eight months. Day by day, we learned the thirty-two letters of the Persian alphabet. The first word we learned was آب. Water. The second word we learned was بابا. Father.

"SPEAK TO ME IN ENGLISH," my father instructed, after I asked him how he was feeling. He took a moment to scan his surroundings, taking his eyes off the board and the mechanical doors to discreetly study individual faces in the crowd. "Don't speak Farsi here. We don't know who could be at this airport."

We were in between seas at the Istanbul Atatürk Airport. So close to a faraway Iran. I was twenty-five. My dad and I were waiting to pick up his family to take them back to our two-week rental: a three-bedroom apartment in the neighbourhood of Aksaray. Eagerly, we awaited Mahin and Haji. This time they were coming with my aunt and uncles. Two of my cousins were joining as well. It was the first time my father would see his two brothers since they'd been teenagers. All three men were now in their fifties.

He had said these words without looking at me. Instead, he stared straight ahead, sweat dripping over his mostly bald head. Focused, he continued to reread the black screen with the little orange lights that listed the arrivals. His eyes darted around as he looked at the people entering through the automatic doors. A young family passed through behind a handful of businessmen. No sign of them.

I had spent the last five years struggling to learn the language he had just rejected.

ONCE WE ARRIVED by taxi to the temporary home that would house our reunion, my dad rolled Haji into the two-person elevator. We began settling into the apartment on the fifth floor, helping Mahin disassemble her luggage. Huge bags of dried mint. Jars of honey wrapped in thick, see-through tape. Tubs of yogourt. Frozen quail meat for dinner. It had all survived two rounds of customs and a one-and-a-half-hour flight.

When the stew was ready, we gathered on the plastic cloth on the ground, leaning our backs against the big brown couches for support. Haji sat a few metres away from us, in his wheelchair in the corner of the living room. The suit he had worn at Pearson was replaced by a white cotton T-shirt and baggy blue pyjama pants that my grandmother had dressed him in. While my father poured the Coca-Cola, I approached my grandfather. I crouched over close and asked, "Haji joon, beldarcheen baa noon mi khaiyeed?" As his health declined, so had his appetite.

"Ye Kam," he replied, squinting and making an empty space with his index finger and thumb. *Just a little bit.* These two words became Haji's slogan over the course of our reunion. I'd ask him if he wanted a drink of water or if he was in pain. He'd reply to me in the same soft voice.

Twenty years after we had first met by translation at the airport in Mississauga, I got just two weeks in Istanbul speaking Farsi to Haji. My favourite childhood story, the one where my homesick father returns to Iran decades later with his only child, remained a myth.

I'M ALMOST THIRTY. It's the end of October and my mother calls to tell me Haji has passed away in Iran. She hands the phone to my father and we cry. The kitchen countertop holds me up. When the call ends, I rush outside to perform living.

My feet speed down Keele Street in pursuit of transit. The hill's incline gives me momentum as I get closer to the station, but something catches my eye to the left of the sidewalk. I slow down and look again.

I see incense sticks growing in the ground. I stop to look closer. They look just like the yellow incense sticks I've used to grieve my mother's parents. The dried-up stems are fixed to the earth. I don't know the name of the plant. I bend my knees further and gaze directly at the shoots of twig breaking out of the ground. They've presented themselves to me in the familiar form of incense to invite me to mourn.

My body has inherited exile and I may never access Iranian soil, but the presence of these plants reminds me of my connection to here. The land is expressing a profound fluency in the language of its migratory kin. I kneel in a place that holds me firmly as I grieve. I can feel the chill of the fall wind, but I remain low to the earth. I close my eyes and place my fingers over my mouth.

Camila Justino

DEAR ENGLISH LANGUAGE

DEAR ENGLISH LANGUAGE,

Sometimes you look at me with this look, as though you know everything. Indeed, you do. Everything is ruled by you. The laws, the signs, and the human thoughts of this land. I try to touch you; you have this nice sound, you are a superstar, the Hollywood celebrities use you, you travel the world performing hit songs that make people cheer even when they don't know you well. Sometimes I wish you were part of me, but you keep being a strange body.

We don't belong to each other. We don't have this intimacy, but still, you are very close to me. You are waves inside my body and you claim and attack my mother tongue for every failure. Sometimes you say particular things in my head:

How could you write using me? You don't know how to channel me.

Then you ask me to stop using you so vaguely, so poorly.

You are an immigrant, you repeat this over and over.

Sometimes you say, You are beautiful, and I am surprised. Suddenly I realize it's not really you, it's the song I listen to on the radio.

You name me an immigrant, and when I am an immigrant I am nothing else.

An immigrant exists to be a character, or to appear on the cover of newspapers (with a suffering face, in an anguished manner, or holding a medal of honour), or on the cover of *The Immigrant Woman Magazine*, or to be part of the statistics (how many of them do we have here?), or to be studied in university, or to be a theme for a conference, or to be helped by non-governmental organizations, or to be interviewed for institutional videos, or to be helped by the church, or to be a beneficiary of governmental budget, or to receive honours on TV, or to be included in politicians' speeches, or to be represented in human rights books. Because I am an outcast, you keep placing me where I'm more convenient. For you. And when I try to defend myself, when I try to say I am not only this, you run away. You put a lot of ideas in my mind and then vanish.

Ha ha! you laugh at me in these moments. I gently gave you this label, you whisper to me. What would you be without me giving you this label? It's for the best—take advantage of being an immigrant.

You are harsh, but then you say I am doing a great job. That was your first reaction when I said one of your level-one sentences in the subway: "Excuse me, I need to get off." You probably say this after feeling sorry for me. You suddenly change, you become polite and try to not compare me to those who are from here, who can use you with fluency. It is easier to feel sorry for me. I accept all your words because I don't know how to argue with you.

I am admired for virtues I will never understand, for leaving my motherland, being a crushed woman with half of my being left in my land, walking around with a broken language as a cane. I am like broken glass, and you put all the pieces together the way you want. You come at night with my tiredness and loneliness, offering a well-done glitter sticker. Because I know how to scrub the floor very well, because I lack language and money.

In the morning, you make me line up for coffee at Tim Hortons. It's important to be functional, you say. Look at all of them. Yes, I agree. They seem ready for work and life. I want to tell you that I don't even know if I like coffee. But you don't listen, you remind me that I wasn't born to write my own stories using you, let someone else do it for me as you are more noble. Get a translator. You keep knocking on me, you are like a serpent, you slither away when I try to speak or write using you. You come and you leave.

Sometimes I try to ignore you. I breathe with relief, and my mother tongue comes back with her warm words, she hugs me but then says it's for the best if she leaves me.

English is not so bad, she tells me, he is objective and also has good humour, he loves you in a different way, but he does love you.

I tell my mother tongue you accuse her of every failure, but she says you have your own reasons.

Do you know tough love? she says with a funny accent.

"Tough love" is an expression that can't be translated into my mother tongue, but she guesses the meaning with her intuition.

Tough love, that's what English feels for you.

She comes to visit me less and less, for my own good. I have saudade, a word followed by a feeling that can't be translated exactly to you, but I can tell you it is a verb that means empty of somebody who fulfills you somehow. Maybe one day you and my mother tongue will get along.

I feel empty. Sometimes I call you or Mother, but you are not there. Why? I have visited this limbo many times, there is no language at all. Where are you guys?

With no language, I use the signs. I pay attention to eyes, mouths, bodies, lines, objects. If they are smiling, I just keep smiling, and follow the tones to survive. I try to be grateful. I know this land is not mine. You gave me permission to live (to survive) here.

Giving me permission to stay in a safe part of the planet is a favour. And an obligation. I am a good argument for human rights.

You both keep providing me with speeches, but when I need you... at least one of you... you are both gone. And why do I need words? I don't like these games. And since my mother tongue left for a while with no sign of return, I am telling you that I am not accepting this anymore.

It took me a while to write this letter. I had these secret words, but I didn't know how to tell you. You will ask: how could I save hidden words from you? I decided to not be your servant anymore.

If you want to stay with me, stay truly. I am owning this space— my brain, my mind, my body. And if you want to fool around or if you want to represent me as a fool, I will laugh at you out loud. I will say, Ha ha, it's not me, it's the English who is fooling around on me.

And don't be surprised if I say words you don't want me to say. Don't feel surprised if I don't repeat things you ask me to repeat.

No, I don't want to be translated in the community centre, or in the doctor's office, and I will not say, *Sorry, I don't speak English.*

I will say, *Sorry, English is learning how to go through me.*

And if you disappear again, I will say, *Sorry, English is gone, you know... he likes to play games sometimes.*

I will not cover your words, your games. Not this time, silly.

I don't want to be represented by a class or by a label chosen by you. I am not just an immigrant. I am not just a woman, a mother, or a man. I am all of it. I am none. I am not a character. I am writing you!

Do you understand, English?

Cheers,

You know who

Amanda Leduc

IT'S JUST A FIGURE OF SPEECH

"There is nothing wrong with calling someone retarded."

It is 1998, and I am sitting in my Grade 11 English class. The speaker is our teacher, a tall, heavyset man with glasses and a gruff German warmth. He is kind to all of us, and his faith in words is absolute.

"*Retard* comes from the French," he says. "*Retarder*—to delay, to be slow. It simply means that someone is slower than average. That's all."

My faith in words is also absolute, but something about this bothers me. I don't know how to say it then. I won't know for many years.

THERE'S NOTHING WRONG *with saying someone has a blind spot. It's literally a fucking spot in the car where you can't see.* A Twitter user says this to me in the spring of 2019, when I put a gentle request out into the world: *hey everyone, please stop using the phrases "tone deaf" and "blind spot" when you're talking about ignorance of something—it's harmful to the blind and d/Deaf/hard-of-hearing communities.*

I am so over this PC language bullshit, the commenter says to me.

I am patient, maybe more patient than I need to be. I am disabled myself and walk with a limp, but not too long ago I used language just like this. I have been there; I know how hard it can be to make this shift.

I stress, again, that my original request is in reference to the use of "tone-deaf" and "blind spot" with regard to ignorance. A literal blind spot in your car is one thing, I tell the commenter, but using this language when you're trying to say that someone is out of touch equates being blind or deaf with being ignorant, and that's simply untrue. To normalize language around this is to place people, however unconsciously, on a hierarchy. To seed the idea that those who are blind and deaf somehow know less than those who are not.

The commenter does not listen. *By the way,* they continue, *I KNOW people with disabilities who've said they have no problem with this phrase. This is utter nonsense.*

Yes? I say, politely. *And I know d/Deaf and blind people who have publicly asked us to stop using this language. What do you lose by taking their wishes into consideration?*

What I did not say then but still think about every day: how important is it for you to have a right to speak when *how* you speak tramples over someone else's right to thrive?

ABLEISM, ACCORDING TO the *Merriam-Webster Online Dictionary*: *discrimination or prejudice against people with disabilities.*

A store without a ramp. A conference with no elevators. An event where the only bathroom is down a long flight of stairs. This is some of what ableism looks like in the physical world: obvious barriers, doors shut straight in the face.

Ableism in language is different—sneaky, mundane, less apt to draw attention. Subtle. Language that draws a connection between various aspects of disability and negative outcomes: *idiot, moron, stupid, crazy, lame, insane. Tone-deaf. Blind spot. Blind to. Turn a blind eye.* Language that—and here's where it gets tricky—purports to draw attention away from disability by pretending it isn't there. *Differently abled, handicapped, handicapable. Special needs.* (The needs of disabled people are not special: they are simply needs that must be met. If you characterize these needs as *special*, then you set up an outcome where meeting those needs is also special, not something to be upset about if it doesn't come to pass. *We tried to meet them and failed. There's nothing else we can do.*)

When we say that someone is *differently abled*, we are saying, instantly, that the abled life is what's regular and proper. We are saying that someone who is *differently abled* can't do some things but can do others, and they should be content to work only with what they have. We are saying that, rather than shifting the world to make opportunities available to all, it's just easier to keep the world as it is and make some people make do with less. But why should a wheelchair user remain on the main floor of a building when the lack of elevators or ramps is what keeps them from accessing another floor? When we say *differently abled*, even in a way that means well, we are saying: *your life only fits into the world a certain way, not the regular way. It isn't society that needs fixing—it's only your body that does.*

(The term itself is also, for the record, just incorrect. Disabled people do not have *special, other* abilities. Life is not a comic book; we don't get to have new abilities just because we don't have others. We don't develop superhuman hearing in response to blindness or amputation. No one gets to be Daredevil, not in real life.)

When we say *differently abled*, we're saying that *disabled* is a bad word. We're saying we don't want to look at what it means to be disabled in the world—to confront the systems that oppress and marginalize disabled bodies.

Ableist language sets up a prison, and from there, a certain way of viewing the world. *She is confined to a wheelchair.* (Because we assume that no one would ever want to be in a wheelchair since the world is not built for wheelchairs. Because we assume that no one would ever find the mobility afforded by a wheelchair magical and freeing.) *He suffers from mental illness.* (Because we cannot conceive of a world in which mental illness is just something you experience— but also, more importantly, because we do not live in a world that has adequate social systems in place for people with mental illness to access the support they need to thrive.)

Ableist language reinforces the idea that there is only one way to be in the world. It does this by propping up systems that are already in place to disenfranchise the disabled body.

What kind of world would we like our language to make?

DO WE SAY *"retard" in regard to other things?* I might have asked my English teacher all those years ago. *If someone finishes last in a race, do we say they're retarded, or they're slower than everyone else? If we avoid using the word in that case, why do we make that decision?*

Is it, perhaps, because we know that the word *retarded* carries something else inside its letters? Something else that has grown with it, a kind of rot that sits deep within its etymological history?

THE WORD MORON was coined by the American psychologist Henry Goddard in 1910. In those days, people with cognitive disabilities were classified in three broad groups: idiot, imbecile, and feeble-minded. An *idiot* was someone with an IQ of between 0 and 25; an imbecile was someone slightly smarter but still lacking heavily in intellectual prowess, with an IQ that ranged from 26 to 50. (*Imbecile:* from the Latin *imbecillus*, also meaning weak-minded.)

A *feeble-minded* person had an IQ of 51 to 70. Goddard felt that the phrase itself wasn't clear, and so he coined the term *moron*, borrowing from the Greek word *moros*, meaning dull. In 1913, to prove his thesis that lower intelligence was linked with crime—because crime, he noted, often seemed "foolish or silly"—Goddard sent his female assistants out to Ellis Island, off the coast of New York City, to interview and recognize the feeble-minded among the immigrant populations. Their "research," such as it was, reported that 40 per cent of the Italian, Jewish, and Hungarian immigrant populations registered as *moronic* under Goddard's system, and the following year many people who registered this way were deported.

Do most people think about this when they call someone a *moron*? Probably not. But the word itself is built around the assumption of unintelligence—we call someone a moron when they have a bad idea, or make a mistake, or believe something that seems ridiculous. (Same goes for those other antiquated terms and their flashier modern versions—in these mid-2020 months of the pandemic, I've heard the phrase *Covidiot* more than I can count.) Because we've been raised to believe, by virtue of the language we use and how it sets up an invisible hierarchy in the world, that to be foolish, to be less intelligent, is something to be afraid of, to be avoided at all cost.

But when you insinuate that a lack of intelligence is a negative thing—when you call someone an idiot, or a moron, or say they are stupid—you are stating that the less intelligent life is a less desirable life, even if you don't think of it in those terms. (Which is to say nothing of the inherent difficulty in measuring intelligence in the first place.)

Nothing is ever *just something that people say*—the words we use all have power, and ableist language is powerful precisely because it hides its harm beneath a veneer of innocuous mundanity, behind the smokescreen of *it's just a figure of speech*. We say that we don't actually think that people who are less intelligent are worthless, but our language reinforces these ideas. And these ideas form the bedrock of our society and determine who is worthy and who is kept out.

LIKE SO MANY others, I didn't think about this until relatively recently. My own journey through language and my ableist unlearnings came about because of disability activists I know and trust—and because my explorations of my own disability, cerebral palsy, uncovered for me how much I too had been guilty of thinking about a disabled life as somehow less than a non-disabled one. I've spent my whole life climbing stairs, even though I have bad balance and am always afraid I will fall, because I was made to understand that stairs were an obstacle I had to overcome. I've never been able to wear high-heeled shoes and I have always been ashamed of this, because high heels are constantly in my face as a symbol of beauty.

Common phrases in the English language privilege the able-bodied life without even thinking about it: you *stand up for* what's right, you *take steps toward* progress, you *walk a mile in someone else's shoes*. What does language like this say to the person who can't stand up, who can't walk, who can't take steps?

It says, however unconsciously, that they—and their bodies—don't belong in the conversation. It is the language equivalent of telling someone they have to take the stairs even if they can't; it communicates the same thing that high-heeled shoes do to those who cannot wear them. It presupposes that there is only one way of moving through the world.

I'M WRITING THIS in the summer of 2020, in the middle of the COVID-19 pandemic. Several weeks ago, a quadriplegic man named Michael Hickson died in Texas from COVID-19. Hickson, who became quadriplegic in 2017 after suffering complications from cardiac arrest, had a wife and five children. He lived in a nursing home, but when he went to the hospital to get treatment for COVID-19, the doctor overseeing Hickson's care was open and blunt.

"So as of right now," he said, in a recording of the call that Melissa Hickson, Michael's wife, shared online, "his quality of life—he doesn't have much of one."

"What do you mean?" she asked, bewildered. "Because he's paralyzed with a brain injury, he doesn't have quality of life?"

"Correct," the doctor said. A third-party organization that had previously been given authority to make medical decisions on

Michael's behalf due to difficulties Melissa had encountered when advocating for her husband agreed with the doctors and made the decision to forego treatment. In Michael Hickson's case, this meant food and water. He died six days after Melissa's phone call with the doctor, his wife never having been able to go in and see him.

While the intricacies of this case are complex, several things stand out to me: the equating of paralysis and brain injury with low quality of life, and the assumption that *no life* is better than a life of low quality. Michael Hickson was undoubtedly in pain, but the mechanisms that underlie the assumption that his life was of low quality are the same mechanisms that we employ when we use ableist language. When abled individuals only ever hear that he was "confined" to a wheelchair, that she was "bed-bound," that he or she "suffered" from one disease or another—without also acknowledging that disabled lives are themselves incredibly complex and have room for joy, no matter how small—it becomes easier to make decisions such as the one that was made for Michael Hickson.

When we use language that posits aspects of the disabled life as less, we posit the disabled body as also less. It then becomes harder for the society we live in to justify the measures we must take to keep these bodies alive—and not only that, but to put in place measures that allow these bodies and these lives to thrive as much as possible. This is why COVID-19 has so terrified the disability community—because choices about the inherent value of a (disabled) life inevitably shape the way treatment is administered.

If his doctors had been influenced instead by language that was inclusive of the ways in which all bodies move through the world, might Michael Hickson still be alive today?

I AM A WRITER: words have always meant the world to me. I love metaphorical language especially—the power that rests in comparing something to something else, in drawing strength from the image of one thing to provide clarity for the other. But I've also been guilty of putting the power of metaphor above the power of harm, of thinking that something will resonate more with my readers if I compare it to something that everyone can imagine. I've used the phrases *blind to* and *wilfully blind* before because I thought they illustrated a point I was trying to make. I used the phrase *that's so lame* in a blog post as recently as five years ago.

But here's the thing about metaphors—they only work if people actually know what they're referencing. Did you know, for example, that only 2 per cent of the world's blind and visually impaired population actually see nothing at all? Most of those who identify as blind or as having a vision loss or impairment see some degree of the world—shapes, colours, or vaguely blurred outlines of the things all around them. When I used *wilfully blind* I conjured up an image for myself of someone intentionally closing their eyes, putting their world into total darkness. But that doesn't actually portray the intricacies of what it means to be blind—to say nothing of the fact that blindness is not a choice, a costume that people can take on and off at will. Thus the metaphor, in the end, did not have the power I wished it to have.

Choosing the power of metaphor here becomes not just a dubious style choice but a cruel one. If I, as a writer, choose to use ableist language without recognizing the harm it can do, then I am continuing to uphold the system that states that the disabled body is worth so much less. Which means I am contributing, however tangentially, to the very real systems that allowed (and continue to allow) people like Michael Hickson to perish.

I don't want to be that kind of writer. I don't want to live in that kind of world.

DO WE WANT language to build us a prison, or do we want language to build us a home? What kind of home would we like ours to be?

Do we want it to be the kind of home where other people feel welcome? Do we want it to be the kind of home that *seems* welcoming at the outset but gradually, insidiously, reveals itself to be a place that might leave some people out of the house entirely?

When you roll your eyes at a dad joke online and say to a friend *that's so lame,* do you think about the fact that *lame* was historically used to reference people with physical disabilities—a limp, a haltering gait—and has, in recent years, come to mean anything undesirable or boring because we subconsciously equate a different way of moving with that which is "undesirable" and "bad"?

When you speak, do you think about the way the history of the words you use presses down into every syllable? Do you stop and wonder if your words are inclusive—if the way that you speak of moving truly encompasses everyone else, or continues to exclude?

I didn't think about this in the past; now it's all I can think about, all I can see.

OF COURSE I *don't think less of anyone when I call them stupid,* people have said to me. *I'm just frustrated! It's just a word that I use! It's a figure of speech!*

But why that word, then—why that choice? I can think instantly of several racist words that many of us (though not all) do not use, precisely because they come with hurtful, negative connotations—words that are loaded with meaning regardless of whether they're used with full intent to hurt or not. We try not to use those words, and there is a wider societal understanding that they are off-limits precisely because they do the same thing: they hint at a hierarchy that places some people above others, that says *these people* and *these bodies* are worth less than these ones. We understand the structural biases built into these words implicitly, and so we try to avoid them.

I think we understand the structural bias in ableist language much less.

I think we *want* to understand the structural bias in ableist language much less. It is easier for the world to operate when it pretends that disabled people aren't here, demanding a seat at the table, because to acknowledge the disabled body is to acknowledge how much of the world needs to be rebuilt, overhauled, made anew. It is much easier to use language that reinforces the idea that disabled people are invisible, not worthy of consideration—because then nothing about the world as we know it needs to change.

As a disabled person, it is one thing for me to hear the insults that someone lobs (*lame, crazy, moron, idiot*) and understand that that person must be ignored—to rise above the hate. It is another thing entirely to face well-intentioned people who don't examine what they say, who hide behind language clichés without understanding their history. Perhaps someone doesn't mean anything by the term *differently abled,* or is trying to be gentle in using a word like *handicapable.* But is language that looks away from disability—and in so doing, away from the structural inequities that disadvantage bodies that are different— really being gentle? Or is it, yet again, being complicit and looking away from a problem that desperately needs to be fixed?

Nothing is ever *just a figure of speech* when the language you use hurts someone else.

SOMETIMES IT'S HARD to believe that that moment in Grade 11 English was over twenty years ago. I think about that teacher—how kind he was to all of us, how clearly he thought he saw the world. So much has happened in the intervening decades that I wonder if he feels like he's moved onto a different planet, if the language that once was home for him has now become alien and strange.

There's everything wrong with calling someone retarded, I might say if I spoke to him now. I hope, as I hope for all of us, that he could grow with that and allow his own language to shift—because when language becomes more inclusive, more aware, we all benefit.

Ayelet Tsabari

DISAPPEARANCE/
MUTENESS

> My Arabic is mute
> choked at the throat
> cursing itself
> without saying a word
> asleep in the airless shelters of my soul
> hiding
> from relatives
> behind the shutters of Hebrew
>
> —ALMOG BEHAR, "MY ARABIC IS MUTE"

There are certain words that always come to me in Yemeni. Words that appear on my tongue without effort. Words that come first, before my dominant languages get a say.

Yemeni Arabic, more specifically, the Judeo-Arabic vernacular of North Yemen, is the dialect my grandparents spoke their whole lives, and my mother and aunts still use when they sing, or when they pepper their Hebrew speech with Yemeni words or quote colourful idioms like "Your rib is broken when you marry off your son; you gain a rib when you marry off your daughter," or imaginative curses like "May the demons kidnap you." The language I heard every time I visited my grandmother, watching her talk with her daughters, her friends, her words accompanied with expressive hand gestures and exaggerated sighs, sounding, always, either mad or cheeky. A language she used for endearments, infused with the love of ancestral mothers, Hayati, Ayuni, Galbi, *my life, my eyes, my heart.* A language I was surrounded by every time I walked the streets of Sha'ariya, the neighbourhood in Israel where she lived, and where my parents grew up. A language I want to believe lies dormant in my body, genetically encoded into my cells, waiting to be awakened, activated. A language I don't speak, and now it is too late. A dying language that, despite its disappearance from the world, managed to take root in my brain in the form of stubborn words that won't let go.

The other day I slipped and twisted my ankle. Except, in my mind, I didn't trip or stumble or ma'adti—the Hebrew word that should have come to mind. When someone in yoga class asked what happened, I eyed her. "Are you Yemeni?" I asked. "Half," she replied, unsure. "Hitgal'abti," I said, pronouncing the throaty ayin as it was meant to sound, as though a marble slides down your throat. Maybe the word stuck because of the mental image it invokes: the way the syllables trip out of my mouth and pile on top of each other. Whatever it is, other words simply won't do.

Hanega, pronounced with a guttural het, is another one of these untranslatable Yemeni words. It comes to me whenever my eight-year-old daughter frowns, pouts, shrugs her shoulders, and refuses to talk. If my siblings or cousins are around, I'd mutter it to them knowingly, the way I'd seen my mother do with my aunts. When I'm with people who aren't Yemeni, the word still rolls to the tip of my tongue before retreating.

I took to Facebook once to consult with other Israeli friends of Yemeni descent about the best way to translate hanega in my work. I was writing a scene for my memoir, in which I used the word to get a reaction from my grandmother. "Are you hanega?" I asked her. She turned to look at me, astonished and pleased to hear me speaking her language.

My post garnered 220 comments and almost as many opinions. "Hanega is not just being offended," observed Ayala, a relative. "It's an entire performance . . . the act of twisting your face and snubbing the offender. Hanega means she won't easily be appeased. It's more than a word or an emotion. It's a cultural story."

I delight in the sound of Yemeni rolling out of my mouth, rejoice in accentuating the letters in that deep, melodic way, feeling as though in my own small way I'm keeping something alive—an endangered language, yes—but also more personally, our past, my childhood, as though in using these words I am channelling my ancestors.

Maybe it also feels like an affirmation, because despite growing up to a Yemeni family, I have often felt not Yemeni enough, was accused of trying to be more Ashkenazi. Was it because I lived in Canada for so long? Was my light-brown skin not brown enough? Or maybe it's because, like many other third- and second-generation Yemenis, I don't pronounce the guttural het and ayins that Mizrahi Jews (or Arab Jews who migrated from Arab lands) were once famous for. That accent, my parents', is still imitated (poorly) and mocked on Israeli satire shows, often by Ashkenazi actors who play Mizrahi characters. Even though it is the accurate pronunciation of Hebrew, which, like Arabic, was meant to have guttural letters. But the country was run by European Jews, so their (incorrect, mispronounced) way of speaking took over and became the norm.

Growing up I liked that I sounded like everyone else, that I fit in. Years later, as I began embracing my Yemeni identity, I regretted not learning this pronunciation from my parents, envied my cousins and friends who did. Now I admire the elegant and musical sound of it whenever I hear it. Sometimes I force it into existence. When reading my Hebrew writing in front of an audience, certain words no longer sound right if the het or ayin are not pronounced; flattening them turns them into different letters, and therefore the words are altered. He'almut, I might say with the glottal ayin. *Disappearance*. Or else, the ayin becomes an alef and the word might sound like Helamut. *Muteness*.

MY GRANDMOTHER NEVER quite took to Hebrew. Arabic always came first, allowed her the range of wit and humour her adopted Hebrew never could. Like most women in Yemen, she was illiterate, but in her sixties, she took Hebrew lessons and learned to sign her name instead of dipping her thumb in ink as she had done before. After her death, I found an official document in my mom's closet: my grandmother's Hebrew given name (which she also never took to) scribbled hesitantly and childlike at the bottom of the page.

My grandfather, like other Jewish men, knew Hebrew from prayers, but that Hebrew was biblical, sacred, not for everyday use. When they arrived in Palestine in the 1930s, Hebrew, which had been a dead language for seventeen generations, became the only way these Jewish immigrants from different countries could communicate. How strange it must have felt to utter these words reserved for prayer in an everyday context, to shop in the market, to argue with a neighbour, to bring them down to earth.

My parents were born into this new language. My mother tells me my father never knew Yemeni, and even if he did, his family spoke the Sharabi dialect, from a different district in Yemen.

"Is it that different?"

"They pronounce *g*, and we pronounce *j*," she said.

How could I expect to speak an ancestral language even my own father couldn't retain?

Many years later, when I came to Canada and had to live in a new language—a language I studied in school but in which I scored a D+ on my matriculation exams, a language that felt unnatural and awkward in my mouth, its long and short syllables like a minefield designed to make me trip (*Don't say bitch when you mean beach,* I prayed every time a visit to Kits Beach was mentioned)—I thought of my grandparents.

THIS IS AN ESSAY about my longing for Arabic, but it is also an essay written in English, by someone who was born into Hebrew, who didn't know English until she was ten, who hadn't read an English book until she was twenty-four, who wrote her first story in English at thirty-three. There are days when I worry that writing in my second language is the most interesting thing about me as a writer. I understand the fascination. Writing in a second language, I had written once, is like wearing someone else's skin, an act akin to religious conversion. This isn't what this essay is about, but how can I ignore that part of my story? That facet of my writerly identity?

I write in English about people who speak Hebrew and Arabic, so it's no surprise that words in these languages demand to be included; they migrate into the English text unitalicized and assert their place in the foreign settings, mirroring my own story of immigration.

After my family and I moved back to Israel in 2018, I got to watch my Canadian partner learning Hebrew, and my daughter, a true bilingual, weaving in and out of tongues, like a basketball player dribbling across the court. "Sometimes it's tiring to live in two languages," she said to me the other day. I sympathize. My eventual mastering of English came at the cost of my Hebrew. Language is a living, evolving thing, and I had been away for twenty years. I used to pride myself on my command of Hebrew grammar; now I am feeling challenged in both languages, a humbling experience that made me rethink my devotion to correct grammar and reconsider what really matters in a work of writing or in daily conversation.

These days, I find myself fearing for my English, again. Whenever my Hebrew flows, I worry my English is at risk. I've seen my mother tongue atrophy; no doubt it could happen to my adopted tongue.

The way we speak at home does not follow any of the recommended rules for raising bilingual children (where each parent must speak only one language). We speak Hinglish, or Ebrew, fluently switch, start a sentence in one language and end with another, and sometimes, mistakenly, we conjugate an English verb in Hebrew grammar. In a sense, the Judeo-Arabic spoken in my grandparents' home was a similar creature. It was the same Arabic their neighbours in Yemen spoke but coloured with Hebrew influences. Later, in Israel, Hebrew became more prominent, but the two were still interlaced, still interplaying.

Moving back to Israel also meant moving to the Middle East, a part of the world largely ruled by Arabic. Palestinian Arabic is in the DNA of this place, and the neighbouring dialects of Egypt, Syria, Lebanon, and Jordan surround us from every border. I grew up watching the weekly "Arabic Movie" every Friday with my mother, an Egyptian melodrama filled with heartbreak, betrayal, and forbidden love. Despite the different dialect, my mom didn't need the Hebrew subtitles. When she went to the kitchen to stir the soup, she asked us to turn it up so she could listen in.

According to research by the Van Leer Institute in collaboration with Tel Aviv University, 10 per cent of Jews in Israel claim they speak Arabic, but only 1 per cent would be able to read a book. The percentage rises significantly, to over 25 per cent, among first-generation Arab-Jews, but drops again with second and third generation.

Mizrahi Jews, some of whom came later than Ashkenazi, faced prejudice and inequity in Israel. Their need to assimilate required an erasure of their past, a denial of their heritage and language, which wasn't just foreign, or diasporic, but also associated with the enemy. Yiddish and other European languages were also lost, but Arabic was more politically charged. Despite sharing roots with Hebrew, which should have made it feel familial, it became viewed as dangerous, and hearing it instilled fear.

Children begged their immigrant parents to stop listening to legendary singer Umm Kulthum (once referred to by an ignorant Ashkenazi reviewer as a screamer), stop speaking Arabic in public. With the exception of the weekly Arabic movie—a source of comfort for many Mizrahi that was reduced to a cult phenomenon by Ashkenazi—Arabic language and culture were not celebrated in the public sphere. The radio didn't play Arabic music, or Hebrew music that *sounded* Arabic, a genre they labelled Mizrahi music. The schools didn't teach our history, our literature. A generation of children were raised to reject their heritage, their language, their parents.

The first time I heard Arabic spoken in Vancouver, instead of feeling nostalgic, I tensed up.

IN 2018, ARABIC was downgraded from an official language alongside Hebrew to a "special status language," a move that caused outrage among Israel's Palestinian population, but also many in the Jewish left, especially those with an Arabic background. In demoting Arabic, the Israeli government made a clear statement about the status of Arabic-speaking citizens in the country.

That's how we ended up a Hebrew-speaking nation shipwrecked in the middle of the Arab world. This is how we ended up living among Palestinians, many of whom (particularly those with Israeli citizenship) speak Hebrew, yet we can't communicate with them in their language. This is how we ended up knowing only the most basic Arabic words, mostly slang and swear words (words that turned Arabic from dangerous to obscene), words we claimed for ourselves, using them casually, carelessly, to the horror of our Arab neighbours.

LANGUAGE BARRIER, A WEB series produced by two fluent Arabic speakers, Eran Singer and Roy Ettinger, both Jewish and Ashkenazi, investigates what went wrong in Israel's education system. They interview experts, visit schools, speak to Jews and Arabs. In one interview, Prof. Muhammad Amara from Beit Berl College says, "Language is not grammar...Language is dialogue. The biggest problem in Arabic language education in Israel is pinned in the fact that they teach it as an enemy language, not the language of the neighbour."

I think of my poor Arabic teacher, a short, unsmiling woman with a thick Iraqi accent, her hair dyed an unnatural black, trying to instill in us an appreciation for her mother tongue. We weren't excited about Arabic, not like we were about English learning. English was sexy. English was Hollywood. English was the future. For those of Mizrahi background, Arabic was the diasporic past we wanted nothing to do with; for everyone, it was a language of war. As homework we listened to Israel's Arabic radio station, learning words like *conflict*, *government*, and *negotiation*. No wonder we lost interest. When the creators of the show enter an Arabic classroom in a Jewish high school, everyone in the room admits they hope to serve in intelligence in the mandatory army, proving Professor Amara's point. In addition, they mainly teach Fusha, Modern Standard Arabic: good for reading but not for speaking. To illustrate this, the producer heads to the market and attempts to buy tomatoes while speaking proper Fusha. "I understood about 80 per cent," the Palestinian shopkeeper replies.

WHEN I WAS THIRTY and living in Vancouver, I got a job waitressing at a Lebanese restaurant. Vancouver had almost no Israelis then, no presence of Hebrew. By then, five years into living in Canada, I no longer tensed to the sound of Arabic. At Mona's I was surrounded by the language, the familiar cuisine, the music. At Mona's my Middle-Easternness was embraced and welcomed. I missed home, and Mona's and the family who ran it gave me one.

My first year at Mona's, I hired Yusuf, an extremely well-dressed Iraqi man I had met there to help me with my Arabic. For some strange reason, I retained my knowledge of the Arabic alphabet, and often drew the rounded, cursive letters on paper when doodling. I recently found a note I had given my partner when we first met a few months after that. Beside my phone number I had written my name in English, Hebrew, and Arabic.

Yusuf was an experienced teacher, and he came to the yellow house I'd been sharing with four roommates off Commercial Drive with work sheets and handouts, complimenting me on my pronunciation and rapid improvement. But he was also way too flirty, and the day I told him so was the last lesson we had together.

I worked at Mona's for six years. After some time, I started taking orders in Arabic, was able to explain poorly and haltingly to Saudi students how much a shish kabob platter cost and what would be on it. I started catching phrases in songs by Amr Diab and Nancy Ajram and was buoyed when I could sing entire lines. Being away from home and its prejudice toward the Arabic language allowed my body to remember Arabic, lament what was lost, and reclaim my own Arabness.

But even at Mona's, surrounded mostly by Canadian Arabs, almost everyone spoke to me in English. My Arabic improved, but then I plateaued.

When I travelled back to Israel to visit, I began researching my Yemeni background, and for the first time used some of these words I'd always known when speaking with my grandmother. In my grandma's last days, I began listening attentively instead of tuning her out. Thinking, here's a word. I know that one. Here's a saying. I have heard this one before. Her eyes beamed whenever I spoke Arabic. The gap between us abridged.

THERE ARE TWO Arabics I long for—my ancestral tongue and the language of this place—or is it really one? Arabic existed alongside my mother tongue for generations, a sister language whose words are often recognizable: bayit and beit, yeled and walad. They share many words, a similar ring, an etymological root, a lingual family, and yet they are estranged. If this is not a parable about the state of this region, I don't know what is.

"Learn Arabic," a Palestinian author I shared the stage with at a literary event in Tel Aviv pleaded with me. "If you moved back here, you owe it to yourself." What she was saying was, it wasn't solely about my own past. It was about our shared future.

On a recent visit to Ushiot, a neighbourhood in Rehovot steeped in the smells of fenugreek and cilantro, where recent immigrants from Yemen live, I heard a child speaking Judeo-Arabic Yemeni. He was maybe six, brown skinned, with side curls and a kippah. He almost looked like the photos I'd seen of Yemeni Jews taken decades ago. His mother was a young woman wearing a head scarf and born in Yemen, a rarity nowadays. The number of Jews in Yemen is in the dozens.

That child may be one of the last people to speak this language. Who will he speak to when he grows up?

Some days I feel a physical ache for Arabic, a tug in my heart. How do you miss something you've never known? Can a language be lodged inside your body, folded into your organs, the same way we inherit memories from our ancestors, like trauma? How else can you explain the warmth that spreads inside my body when I hear it? The yearning?

I WANT THIS ESSAY to have a happy ending. I want to tell you I signed up for Arabic lessons at the community centre. Which I did, but then COVID shut it down before classes began. I want to tell you I enrolled my daughter in one of those few and rare Jewish-Arab schools, where kids study in both languages. My partner and I went to visit one in Jaffa before she started first grade. Children ran around, playing in two languages, shifting back and forth seamlessly. "I'm sorry," the principal said. "You must live in the district to enroll."

What I *will* tell you is that I recently learned my memoir will be translated into Arabic, and how deliriously happy this made me; I'd been dreaming of being translated into Arabic. And then—how deeply sad, because I knew I couldn't read it myself.

I MAY NOT SPEAK ARABIC, but these days I sing in Arabic.

When I discovered the Yemeni Women's songs a few years ago—a repertoire of songs women sang at henna ceremonies, at births and weddings, a form of oral storytelling that had been passed on, unwritten, for generations, now on the verge of disappearance, of muteness—I wanted to learn them theoretically, through listening. Then I realized this wasn't enough. I needed to join the singing, to become an active participant in the tradition of passing the songs on.

I see my teacher, Gila, at her home in a small moshav by Jerusalem. We sit in her living room, or on the balcony facing fields and hills. She teaches me the songs and their translation and tells me of their history and meaning. When I sing, my mouth does not stumble, even as it mimics words it doesn't know. The translation is there, but when I sing, I rarely look at it. Singing is its own language. Before the pandemic, Gila even suggested I accompany her to sing at a henna. I don't know if there's anything more affirming than this.

The other day, as I was practising the songs, my daughter inched forward until she stood next to me. Then her small voice joined in, imitating the foreign words. Her body knew what it was supposed to do too. As we sang, I tried to be still, to not disturb the moment. We sang and I could hear our ancestors singing along with us.

Carrianne Leung

THE REACH

anguage, to me, has always been about reaching. I have never "belonged" in language. There have been moments when I have found refuge, but language is a shifting ground, a churning sea, and never a place for me to land.

My maternal grandmother was also a writer. She wrote serial love stories under a pseudonym that were in syndicated newspapers in the 1930s and 1940s in Hong Kong. No one in my family knows much about this part of her life or seems to care, even as I find it extraordinary.

When she was already old, and I was a child, I would file her nails and inhale her—the smoke from her menthol cigarettes, the camphor of the white flower oil and the talcum powder she liberally sprinkled on her skin after a bath. I remember these small gestures, these small moments, these small silences. She was a woman trapped in a Scarborough house in the late seventies, captive to a foreign language she didn't understand and white faces that did not give a damn about her. But at night, I was at her side.

When I was five years old, I emigrated with my family from Hong Kong to Canada. My ability to speak Cantonese was interrupted, my tongue arrested and frozen in childhood. My parents, both fluent in English and wanting me and my brother to master it, didn't enforce Cantonese at home. We settled on the "Chinglish" so familiar in other diasporic households. I never learned how to write or read. This was the first loss. Years later, as a young adult, I would return to Hong Kong to live, and I fumbled to find words again. While my face allowed me entry to an optics of belonging, my capacity to express myself in Cantonese betrayed me every time. My stuttering tongue, the long pauses in conversations, as I tried frantically to search for the right word or phrase in my head, my tones a bit off when I got nervous, and that childlike vocabulary always raised the flag that I might not be what I seemed. There were the telltale signs of a profound loss. In the three years I lived there, Cantonese would always be a hard stretch, but one infused with joy when I found connection with the right word, the right time, and the right person. It's a colourful language, full of vernacular, rich with vocabulary. I would sometimes find a place to sit. It could be a mall or a park or a street market. I would close my eyes and get lost in the sounds of the language around me and be soothed. Language is more than words, syntax, meaning; it is reverberation, it is energy, it is visceral.

As a child immigrant, while Cantonese receded from my life in Canada, I found English, and I also found silence. To me, English and silence are interwoven because I learned them at the same time.

My life was divided between Hong Kong and life after. Immigration cleaved and transformed me. I went from a chatty rascal of a child to a silent and still one. At an event, recently, I was asked what I was like as a child, and I replied that I was silent. I became the quintessential quiet Chinese girl. The one who became invisible, blended into the background, docile, easily managed. I figured out quickly that I did not belong—that no one looked like me, played like me, or sounded like me. When I watched that *Sesame Street* skit, "one of these things is not like the other," I understood that this was me. I was not like the others, and everybody else knew it too.

But then my silence grew into something else, something rich and thick and full of nuance. Silence floated around me, and I could easily pluck at it and shape it, disappear into the place inside, where Cantonese was fading and English was flooding in. Silence was where things formed in between language and contained all my wanting, my fears. It could hold all the things I could not quite name—what was happening to me, my loneliness, the splendour of what I saw too. Silence did not let me down. As a writer, I chase after silence and try to capture it in words, knowing I will always fail. I do it anyway because it's in the silence that everything I want lives.

I learned English because I discovered books as a kid. I had been too young to acquire literacy in Chinese, so English was where I discovered the written word. I owe a great debt to Jean Little. My school library carried her books, and these books became friends. They did not require me to speak but only to listen. Little found a way to put the pain and loneliness of children into language and offered me vocabulary to connect to my own experience. There is such spaciousness offered when a reader connects with a writer through the word. From then on, I saw possibility.

I still grab at the possibility of language, but I know there will never be mastery over it. I suppose I have gained some accomplishments. I have written a PhD dissertation, two books of fiction, various academic and personal essays. I have fluency, but fluency only means I have mastered a level of syntax, mode of address, communities of lexicon. There are times when I am called to speak or write, and I still stutter. I still stumble.

This comes from knowing that I work in a language and discourse where I will always need to reach. When I reflect on "writer's block,"

I discover that it is a reach back into silence. I lost a language I was born to inherit. Simultaneously, I acquired a language that was not for me, but that I learned to bend into shapes that suited me. But mostly, I dwell in silence, a secret language that is misaligned and mistaken for complacency, void, inaction.

Silence is and has functioned as an active historical practice against BIPOC bodies. Silence has a lineage, if you will. Silence is also its own language. So, you see, silence is many things—both our oppressor and our craft. This is the tricky thing about writing in a colonizer's language.

I also know the act of finding language to speak comes with the labour of pulling from blood and bone. Writing is my insistence. But sometimes, even when I am able to break the surface and come up with the words, it is not enough. As Dionne Brand reminds us in the title of her book of poetry, "no language is neutral." The terms of engagement can also erase all that I try to make. I spend a lot of time trying to find language. The words need to be exact and yet open, dynamic and yet heavy. They have to be sharp like the points of arrows, and beautiful too, like sparks of light on a lake.

But sometimes it's not the words, not their careful craft, arranged precisely in intricate patterns. Sometimes it's not the words that are at fault for why they don't land where and how they should. It's up to the reader to reach too, and at times the reader will simply not let the words pierce and settle. This is often what confronts BIPOC writers. We know the enormity of what we are writing against. The readers are sometimes locked in their own world of mythology. This narrative that arrives from my body may already be at odds with the reader's mythology.

Knowing the stakes, I love words too much to declare them my enemy, and so I reach. My practice as a writer is simple—make the space, make it large with intention and care, braid all our languages together, articulate a new world. What choice do I have?

My grandmother died on my thirtieth birthday. I had read somewhere that Confucius says at age thirty one must take a stand. I knew my grandmother was sending me a message—the most important one, and so this gold thread is what knits my spine together, and she is also what I reach for when I write my stories.

Janet Hong

RELEASE MY TONGUE

have a complicated relationship with Korean. Call it what you want—mother tongue, native tongue, birth language—but whenever I am asked about this relationship and its implications on my work as a translator of Korean literature and as a writer writing in English, something inside me stops short. For most of my life, I didn't question this resistance, this ball of yarn, growing more and more knotted at the core of myself. I accepted it as natural, simply part of my emotional makeup. It was only in my fortieth year, in the history-making year of 2020, that I began the painstaking journey of unravelling the snarls.

I was born in Korea, and Korean was the only language I knew until my father's job required my family to move to Seattle, USA, where we lived for almost a year, and then to Vancouver, Canada, where I attended kindergarten. As a kindergartner, I was exposed to a minuscule amount of English, compared to the Korean I spoke and heard at home. While my English instruction wasn't enough for me to effectively pick up the language, it was enough to make me realize I was different, that I did not belong.

In my kindergarten there was a girl named Laura, a pretty girl with light brown hair. I think we were friends, or I wanted to be her friend. In one memory, a group of us are on our way out of the classroom. I call out to Laura, who is walking ahead. She stops and turns, her mouth set in a grin. "It's Lau-*ra*, not Lau-lah," she says with a giggle. I try, awkwardly curling my tongue to make the proper "r" sound, but my tongue is thick and stubborn. I try again. Amusement bubbles in the eyes of my classmates. "No, it's Lau-*rrrra*," she repeats, and my heart sinks. I don't think she's trying to be malicious; she is pointing out differences as children tend to do, but I remember the strain of my tongue, the suspicion that there was perhaps something fundamentally different about the composition of our tongues, and how, in the end, her name sat heavy and dull in my mouth, like a stone.

A sense of estrangement lingered, following me even when my family moved back to Korea toward the end of the school year. Though I was no longer considered foreign, I'd been marked by otherness, and my understanding of myself had changed. Except this time the shame of estrangement had morphed into pride—something I now recognize as privilege.

Everything changed once more when I was eight, when my family immigrated to Canada for good. At my new elementary school, there were several recent immigrants who were Korean. They approached me on the schoolyard and addressed me in our native language, their words piercing through the fog of English. Vancouver wasn't nearly as culturally diverse then as it is now, and so, meeting another Korean—even a perfect stranger—had the same effect as running into a relative. Though I felt instant kinship with the Korean students, to hear the language of home on their tongues, I felt something else too—a kind of guilt, a flush of shame. I could see that our mother tongue marked us as outcasts.

When you live in a country where you don't speak its language, not only are you cut off from understanding, but you're also unable to make meaningful connection. A silence grows within you, until you become sealed in silence, and this—the thought of being unseen, of being unheard—I couldn't bear. The best thing I could do was to assimilate, and the key to assimilation was to learn English. And not just learn it, but achieve "native" fluency, or better yet, master it. Instinctively I understood that for this to happen, every trace of my previous accent had to be wiped out. It seemed unrealistic, maybe greedy, to think I could be equally at home in Korean and English, and so I told myself I had to choose one, at the cost of the other, since they would always be competing for dominance. I needed to banish my mother tongue and let English win.

I wasn't the only one thinking along these lines. My mother, on my English tutor's recommendation, packed away our Korean books and movies and replaced them with English ones. We stopped visiting friends who had recently emigrated from Korea, and she, in not so many words, encouraged me and my brother to make "Canadian" friends instead. The only Korean we used during this time was at home with one another, and more out of necessity. If they'd had a choice, they probably would have spoken English to us. Their tactic: to subdue our mother tongue so that our second tongue could flourish. The last thing on their minds was the possibility that our mother tongue could erode away.

I impressed everyone with the rapid pace at which I picked up English, and by the end of elementary school my assimilation was complete. I took pride in my accent-free speech and the fact that I had gained "native speaker" status. All the while, I was losing my mother tongue, but I hardly noticed or cared.

Now, you have to understand: I was the kind of child who would get choked up with emotion at the first strains of the Korean anthem, one who could rattle off the list of Korean medals won during the Seoul Summer Olympics of 1988, one who dreamed of making some meaningful contribution to the country of my birth.

Surrendering my mother tongue was akin to betrayal, to denying the core of who I was. And so, to paraphrase the words of Madhu H. Kaza from her book *Kitchen Table Translation*, a vital part of me went silent when I arrived in Canada. I imagine it as a garden that becomes overgrown with disuse, silent, the gate hinges rusted with neglect. My inner life became tied in knots, growing twisted into a tangle I'm recognizing only now as grief.

AS I PROGRESSED through school, my desire to "master" English became a genuine love for the language, and I started to dream of becoming a writer. I began thinking of English as a language of literature, a language conducive to complex emotions and thoughts, while Korean was relegated to a language of childhood—a language of home and food and family, one for communicating basic needs. (On a side note, this is reflected in my voice, even now. When I speak English, my voice is deeper and I am more confident, but when I speak Korean, my voice becomes higher-pitched, like a child's, and my sentences often end in a questioning tone.)

I wanted to write books like the ones I read. I didn't want to write about the Asian experience, just because I was Asian, and I resented the expectation that I should be writing about the "immigrant literature." I even considered adopting an anglophone pen name. I wanted to erase my Korean identity, to hide the fact that I was writing in my second language.

Around the same time, my love for literature, which I read only in English, made me curious about the literature of my heritage. And so, on a lark, in my third year of university, I enrolled in a Korean language course where the final project was to translate a Korean short story into English.

It turned out I had a certain knack for translation. Translation gratified my urge to write, since I was the one coming up with the right combination of English words and there isn't one way a work can be translated into a language. But more than that, I found that the process of turning Korean words into English ones was not unlike the "translation" I had put myself through when I first immigrated to Canada. I submitted that first piece to a translation competition hosted by the *Korea Times*, and when I ended up receiving the grand prize, my career path seemed decided.

In her poem "Search for My Tongue," Sujata Bhatt writes that every time she fears she has lost Gujarati, her mother tongue, it comes back stronger, more tenacious, like a vine that will not die.

Perhaps I couldn't resist the pull of my native language. Perhaps my mother tongue, buried and dormant until then, was also biding its time to assert itself.

SEVERAL YEARS LATER, as an MFA student in creative writing, I was working on a collection of short stories, but my mentor thought they lacked depth. I'd been so conscious about resisting the pressures about writing about my identity that I'd gone to the other extreme and removed every trace of race from my characters. And herein lay the contradiction: while as a translator I was championing Korean voices, as a writer I was still preoccupied with erasing my Korean Canadian identity.

I realized I wasn't emotionally invested in the collection. I threw the whole thing out and began to write, without an outline, without thinking about my thesis or graduation or other people's expectations. What sprung out was my childhood—my inner life and secret memories, the many losses I'd felt as a child, the grief of losing my father in my last year of high school. Though my manuscript was in English, these stories were littered with Korean words and phrases. I agonized to find English equivalents, and if I did manage to come up with translations, they were poor shadows. In the end, I felt compelled to leave many words in Korean. Even now, I see them as outposts in an alien land, their small lights flickering in the darkness of the night.

AFTER I GOT MARRIED and moved to Toronto, there were even fewer opportunities to use Korean, aside from the smattering of words and phrases I sometimes used with my Korean Canadian partner, or at the Korean market or restaurant. But my mother tongue still slips out when I least expect it.

In the fall of 2015, I was accepted into a writing residency at the Banff Centre. There I met an Argentinian writer with whom I felt an intense kinship. One evening we continued to drink in the common room late into the night, after everyone had headed back to their rooms. Drunk, I found myself blurting Korean words to her. Yen-na-rae... sa-rang... I ended up playing for her an old Korean pop song, a song released the year before I immigrated to Canada. I must have heard my parents playing it over the years, but it had become mine somehow, evoking a knot of emotions and nostalgia within me. I translated each line for her in sloppy, maudlin English, and by the end we were both laughing and weeping.

Standing in the shade of a roadside tree, I see your face in front of me... Ah, beautiful world, don't let me forget how I loved... The trees are thinning now, but the scent of lilacs is growing stronger...

What is it about the mother tongue that comes back to assert itself when I let my inhibitions go, when I feel an especially strong connection to someone? What does it mean when I involuntarily revert to the language of my childhood, after having repressed and censored it for almost thirty years?

IN THE FALL OF 2019, I had the opportunity to spend a month in Korea as LTI Korea's translator-in-residence. Though I'd travelled to Korea a number of times for work, this was the first time my family was joining me, and the first time my two children, then seven and four years old, had set foot in the country.

I was excited to introduce my family to where I'd been born, and to the many relatives they'd never had a chance to meet. Though I didn't voice it, I secretly hoped this stay would prove magical; that, by subjecting my children to a constant stream of Korean, their ears would be opened and my sense of failure for not having made more of an effort in their bilingual education would be righted.

But once there, I found my children ignoring whoever was speaking to them, not bothering to cast them a glance. This dismissive behaviour was very much unlike them. Finally I clued in. Their grasp of Korean was so thin they simply weren't able to tell they were being spoken to.

The fact that this came as a surprise seems almost foolish. How could I have been so unaware? But it surfaced a more disturbing, personal question. How is it that I, a translator who directly benefits from multilingualism, have neglected to instill in my children the importance of knowing Korean? No, "neglected" isn't the right word. Neglect implies a slip of the mind, something you might mean to do, but forget in the end. For a person in my line of work, not raising their children bilingually is not only extremely unusual, but perplexing.

Actions often reveal what lurks in your heart, the hidden motives you might not be ready to confront or accept. It's not that I didn't value Korean. Of course I did. No one needed to convince me of its beauty, its power, its plasticity.

Because of the nature of my work, people assume that I feel at home in both Korean and English. Most of the time, it's true, I feel accepted by the worlds the two languages represent, but there are just as many times when I feel like an outcast in either language. Even though English is my dominant language, there is always a sense I am performing. There is a pressure not to make mistakes, to get it right, and to get it right each time. I constantly second-guess myself and obsess over my words. I work with an online dictionary and thesaurus open on my browser. I nitpick, I fiddle, I scrutinize, I am full of doubts.

Growing up, I learned many English words through books, instead of hearing them spoken at home or at school, and so naturally there were quite a few I pronounced incorrectly. To this day, I still cringe to think about these mistakes. How, in the seventh grade, I'd meant to say the colour "taupe" but instead said "toupée," making a classmate laugh so hard that tears ran down her cheeks. Or how I'd once talked about an "excavator," but called it an "ex-*kav*-i-tor," with the stress on "kav." Or probably my most cringe-worthy moment of all: how during one translation seminar, in the presence of my professors and fellow students, I'd been describing a certain texture and had referred to a pumice stone, except I'd called it a *pyoo*-mis stone—the way one would pronounce "pubic." I'll never forget the shock on everyone's face, followed by one girl's—my rival's—correction and gleeful cackle. These blunders—I'll never live them down.

No, I hadn't neglected to teach my children Korean. I was instead trying to save them from the doubts and anxieties that plague me. I wanted to give them a life free of insecurity. I didn't want them to feel like imposters, haunted by an aura of illegitimacy. Just as my mother believed she was giving me and my brother what we needed when we'd first immigrated, I'd made a subconscious decision to give my children what I thought was best: belonging.

JUST AS ENGLISH is my dominant language, despite Korean being my first language, translation has become my dominant endeavour, though I began with writing. Writing is what I studied, not translation, and becoming a writer was a long-time dream, before it even occurred to me that one could translate as a profession. Still, translation is what I spend most of my time doing, and writing is something I never have time for.

If I sound ungrateful, I don't mean to. Translation is undoubtedly one of my passions, and I cherish the fact that I have the privilege of bringing important voices to anglophone readers. Every time a new translation of mine receives a great review or is nominated for an award, I'm elated, as if a book I'd written myself has been recognized. But just like my two languages, my two practices—writing and translation—are at war with one another, wrestling for control. With the publication of every new book I've translated, and with each passing year my novel-in-progress continues to languish on my computer, it appears that translation has triumphed, which, when I stop to let the truth sink in, breaks my heart.

Could it be that I feel guilt for abandoning my mother tongue, for having assimilated, for having chosen English, for my privilege? Could it be that I'm paying for it now, by burying my own stories? Could it be that my writing is just dormant, waiting to grow back when I'm least aware, waiting for night to come so it can grow shoots and strong veins?

EIGHT YEARS AGO, around the time my husband and I moved back to Vancouver from Toronto, I went to a new dentist for a routine checkup. During the examination, he mentioned something no one had ever told me before: I had a minor tongue-tie. It explained why I couldn't roll my "r's," why my tongue was shorter compared to those of others. But since my speech wasn't affected and I'd lived my whole life without any discomfort, there were no medical reasons for me to get it cut.

From that point, however, I started wondering how it would feel to have "normal" tongue movement like everyone else. I wondered, is this why certain words seemed to require more effort to pronounce? I also discovered this surgery was referred to as having one's tongue-tie "released." I got it into my head that I would like to have it done, and so early last year, the year I would turn forty, I received a frenectomy.

To be honest, I haven't experienced any life-altering, or even minor, changes. My tongue, when I stick it out, is barely longer, and the strain, when pronouncing certain words, isn't any less—not that I experienced major difficulties before. However, around the time I was considering surgery, I was invited to contribute to this *Tongues* anthology. Shortly after, I participated in a conversation about the mother tongue for a literary translation conference organized by the PEN America Translation Committee. Maybe I'm just hardwired to search for deeper meaning and hidden connections, but while getting my tongue-tie released may not have been physically necessary, symbolically it seemed of the utmost importance.

A lingual frenectomy is performed to free the tongue and allow it a greater range of motion. All my life, my two tongues—Korean and English—and my two passions—writing and translation—have been pitted against one another. If one rose, the other fell; if one fell, the other rose. The entire process has been characterized by effort and strain. Ah, now I see what this has been about. I'd said a sense of belonging, above all, is what I wanted for my children, and in some ways, it's true. But maybe what I wanted for them was a life free from striving, from doubt, from insecurity. A life free of the burden of constantly weighing their words. I wanted them to step into the world, at least this part of the world, secure and carefree, and see it unquestionably, undoubtedly, as their home. It's freedom I've been after all along.

During the months we were stuck at home at the start of the pandemic, I taught my oldest child how to read Korean. It may take him a while and he may not understand what he's reading, but now he can sound out the letters. These are small steps, I know, but they are enough for the moment. Instead of subjecting my children to my anxieties about Korean, making them swallow one new word after another, I will let them be, and hope the seeds of this tongue, cast so long ago, will find a way to sprout when the time is right.

Danny Ramadan

SPEAK MY TONGUE

t's one o'clock in the morning and I'm tired. Matthew and the three or four remaining guests are in the living room, and I smile as I hear their laughter. I'm sneaky. I grab the speakers' remote control and lower the volume gradually, every minute or so, until Dolly Parton is hushed in her desperate pleas to Jolene. Someone demands more tequila, and I open a cupboard and stash the bottle there, regretfully informing the group that we have run out. The neighbours might put up with a birthday party, but I know their patience is thin. Matthew walks into the kitchen and holds me close, whispers a quick thank-you to me for planning this party for him.

"Of course, babe, I adore you," I say, while doing the dishes, trying not to smash a wineglass. "Your happiness is the world to me."

He pauses, and I smile. He must be emotional. "Babe, you're drunk," he says, and I realize I have been casting stones in my head while I'm equally wasted. "You're speaking to me in Arabic."

IT'S 3:30 A.M. and the winter is howling outside like a pack of wolves. My nightmare stays with me after I wake up, and I feel triggered by an intensely violent memory. I know how to handle this, I think to myself, and I start attempting to fill my head with positive thoughts. When I'm triggered, I can't feel my body anymore—it's a foreign land.

The only parts of my body I feel are the tense muscles in the base of my neck. I want to rub them, but my hands are still back in the nightmare. I hear Matthew ask if I'm okay and I whimper. He wakes up and starts massaging the back of my neck; this feels nice. He is saying things to me, calming things. His voice is sweet; it echoes in my soul.

For the life of me, though, I can't seem to understand a word he says in English—my brain is too foggy to navigate his words. Too shackled to translate his words into my primary language in my head.

IT'S 8:30 P.M. and they're not born yet. My child is in bed trying to trick me into staying up for one more minute, and I insist it's time for them to fall asleep. I see myself older, my salt-and-pepper hair perfectly curly, as I always envision it being in my older days.

I KNOW THIS CHILD of mine is not going to be my biological child. I have promised my future child that they will not inherit my collective traumas. I have promised them I will be a better father than my own dad and a better mother than my own mother. I promise their unborn soul that they will be loved. I also promise that they will inherit my heritage. They will carry my story and the stories of my ancestors. They will be Assyrian, like me—and will speak Arabic, like me. I promised them to learn about whatever racial identity they came from and teach them about it too. They will be a beautiful mix for our modern family.

In my head, I pull the fairy tale book of Kalila and Dimna from a shelf and start reading to that child of mine, in my velvety Arabic words, stories of jackals and elephants and kings of forests. I even do voices. That unborn child of mine will love me doing voices.

I want Matthew to learn Arabic and he knows it. He knows it's important to me because it's my language of love, the language I want to hear when I need comforting, and he has come to see how important it is to me that our future children feel this connection to my roots in their upbringing.

Learning Arabic is not an easy task, I admit. Statistically, Arabic is the second-hardest living language to learn after Japanese. Also, the fact that our alphabet is Semitic, while English, French, and German—languages he speaks to various degrees—are all Latin languages. Finally, English is a small language, meaning the word pool of English is limited to around six million words, while Arabic's word pool is an ever-expanding 560 million words.

"How do you say *walk* in Arabic?" Matthew asks me.

"Well, it depends! Where are you walking from? Where are you walking to? Which direction are you taking? Are you going west or east? How are you feeling as you walk? Are you walking softly with joy in your step, or walking fast with anger in your head?"

"Okay, okay, I get it: Arabic is hard."

Sometimes I wonder if it's fair to ask him to learn Arabic. I speak English fluently, and even when I mispronounce an English word, there is enough love in our relationship to see that as a joyful moment of laughter. I spoke English fluently before I met Matthew, I didn't learn the language for him—although I have met other couples where one partner had to learn English to communicate well with their spouse.

I also ask myself if it's fair to compare languages to begin with. Languages carry with them not only a way of communicating but also culture, song, dance, metaphors, and tradition. Even the voice I use when I speak English is different; English is a nasal language that's high-pitched, while Arabic is a language born in the throat with rolling *r*'s and spitting *kha*'s.

Even in their ways of describing the same things, the two languages are vastly different. I find it beautiful that in Arabic when you feel joy, you say that your heart is turning to ice, while in English you say that joy warms your heart. It's not fair to compare one expression to the other: what's fair is to see both expressions for what they carry in subtext—an intimate tie that tells you about the environment these expressions were born in and the people they represent.

I don't believe the issue here is communication: Matthew and I communicate wonderfully. I believe languages represent a way of connection and bonding. There will always be a part of who I am and where I come from that will not be revealed to Matthew unless he learns Arabic. A heritage that will not pass down to our children unless we both connect to it in our own essence.

The global dominance of English as the prominent language of communication is rooted in colonial practices and cultural occupation. Our personal relationship—essentially, our love—is impacted by the supremacy of English, whether we like it or not. Unless we pay close attention to it, we will always communicate well, but will we be able to connect? I would love for our relationship to be a practice in respecting each other's heritage and the depth of our connection to a land and a tongue.

A final story: I tiptoe into the bedroom. Matthew is already asleep and I slip out of my clothes and into bed next to him. He mumbles something and I smile. I rest my hand on his side and he turns around, smiles to me, and whispers, "Hello, murderous humanoid."

I smile and tell him to go back to sleep. The next morning, we laugh about this. I post about it on Facebook and our friends laugh.

In a year, I will be sitting around a dinner table with his mother and brother, sleep-talking will come up, and I will tell this story. One day in our late fifties, he will be joking with me and he will call me a murderous humanoid in an ominous voice.

I wonder how many times I have woken up in the middle of the night and whispered something so meaningful, so funny, or so dark to him in Arabic. I wonder how many times he smiled but did not understand.

Sadiqa de Meijer

MOEDERTAAL

i.

My mother's vowels were as clear as drinking water. She expected ours to sound the same. She was a teacher, the child of two teachers; before them, there was a madwoman, a sea captain, a divorcée, a drunk. And then blacksmiths, generations of them, clanging out horseshoes on inherited anvils.

"The finest Dutch," she used to say, "is spoken in Haarlem." That wasn't where we lived.

I thought of the song about the bells.

The clocks of Haarlem, they sound sweet of tone.

The Dutch words for sound (the verb) and vowel are very close: *klinken* and *klinker*. The bricks of the old streets are also called *klinkers*, which has to do with the archaic term *inklinken*, to shrink down or dry or compress a material.

WHEN I WAS in first grade, our class visited an abandoned brick factory on the Rijn. We knew the ruined structure as the backdrop to a quarry. People swam there in the summers. Our cupped hands, plunged in the shallows, would emerge crowded with wriggling tadpoles. *Dikkopjes*: little fatheads.

The building that had manufactured bricks was also made of bricks: one tall round chimney, a row of arched ovens with crumbling walls, and a roof overgrown with dandelions. Our guide had worked at the factory. The river clay, he explained, had been dug from where the quarry now was, then purified and shaped and baked. He told us the quality of bricks can be confirmed by listening for their lucid, musical pitch when banged together.

WE WERE FROM schoolteachers, and we would sound like it.

Not from market vendors, who spoke the Dutch of our region: grammatically pragmatic, lower in pitch, with languidly melodic tones. That was called flat. It had to do, a long time ago, with the elevations of the land.

And also not from the queen, with her architectural hats, her bruised and reticent inflections. That was talking with a hot potato in your mouth.

What a tough and lovely feeling it was to slip into the vernacular on the streets. To skin a knee and pronounce "I'm bleeding" as "I bloom."

MOTHER TONGUE. IN HER book on the subject, Yasemin Yildiz warns us against the term's implied assumption that a first language carries an "affective and corporeal intimacy."[1]

Oh, but it is indeed my mother tongue.

My pulse music, my bone resonator, my umbilical ligature.

"The milk language," says Ghita El Khayat, who published *Le Petit Prince* in its first dialectal Arabic translation, "because such a story is a gift from mother to child."[2]

My language of the lullaby and nursery rhyme.

My language of the effortless diminutive, the suffix *je*, which in the vocabulary of early childhood, when doorways and hedges and grown-ups towered over us, seemed to permeate our portion of the world:

dutje, kusje, laarsje, kindje   nap, kiss, boot, child

And when I stood on the low plaster toadstool that served as a trail marker in the woods near Ede, still too small to get there without someone lifting me or to leap off without clutching their hand, it was the language of first namings: *boom, grond, lucht.*

ARE THERE ANY spoken sounds as elemental? Not to my ear, not to the anvil bone of my inner ear.

Boom, grond, and *lucht* exist where I live now as well. Trees, ground, and sky.

The ground is not that old ground; it is another continent.

The sky is continuous with the old one, but it feels different. It isn't as vast and fresh, or as haunted by hurried clouds. Here the people do not call it *lucht,* and so it isn't also air, which means it is impossible to breathe this sky.

Sky cannot fill your lungs or flow into your bloodstream.

Only the *lucht* can do that.

ii.

Dutch is not the name of my language.

Dutch, that crushed stone, that steaming pressure-cooker valve—there is no resonance in that disintegrating syllable, Dutch, Dutch, Dutch; its closest correlate is *Duits,* which means German, which is altogether different, with its cragginess and hushings and reverently capitalized nouns.

The language I speak is Nederlands, NAY-*der-lahnts,* in three descending pitches: of the low land; low or humble or meek, as in the Sermon on the Mount, for they shall inherit the earth.

The utterances of my people, who used to dwell on hillocks, lone islands in the floodplains of the sea. And they had never heard of Christ.

When the tide was high, their houses looked like anchored ships.

In storms, the rain and whitecaps lashed their walls. Was it any wonder that the words they made would sound like phlegm? Their grooved hands gathered frigid peat and dried it in the wind to make the slabs that fuelled fires. Rainwater was stored, for drinking, in a hole outside the door.

That is my language, of wind moving over earthen homes in shallow seas, of a vessel dipped in a rainwater pit, of a cough from a straw bed.

Grammar of nettles and elderberry and the blue-grey shells of blackbird eggs. Of windbreaks of knotted willows. Of rivers that flood the fields and freeze. Irregular verb of the wooden skates, the scrape of blades that herringbone the ice, the sensation of flying toward the flat horizon.

CONSONANTS ARE LAND; vowels are water.

My speech of the sluiced and siphoned vowels. Of the proper vowels in straight trenches. Of the stubborn vowels that will not stop seeping through the clay.

CROWDED SYNTAX OF BICYCLES, released with the green light, a wheeling cluster that crests like a wave over an old arched bridge. The chirp of the signal for pedestrians with visual impairments, the swoosh of plastic rain-pant legs, the lingering, quietly stale flavour of coffee, and the salty aftertaste of bami goreng. Plosive of a glass jar landing in the communal recycling dumpster.

Disappearing dialects of fine terroir; of cities, twenty minutes apart, with distinct municipal accents. The verbal tunes of Drenthe, of Limburg, of Zwolle and Brugge and Rotterdam.

MY VOCABULARY OF images from a train at dusk; a reel of domestic scenes in the apartments near the tracks. A newspaper held wide by an unseen reader, an old man without a shirt, two children looking out. The clatter of the elevated rails.

Then indigo countryside, and one rural house, a solitary square of light.

That script of intimate and irretrievable moments in rooms, of living Polaroids, embedded in an immense and deepening darkness.

I SPEAK THE LANGUAGE of the train, and those apartments, and that house.

The syllables of apartment stairwells that smell of ammonia, of a thin lawn where a woman in curlers holds the leash of her tiny dog, of a snack bar where the air is thick with deep-fryer fumes.

The diction of the lone house, with its straw roof and tile floors, the neighbouring medieval castle with a moat. Of waking to the calls of mourning doves and distant cows, taking warm eggs from the dim chicken coop, inhaling a forest of bark and acorns and mushrooms, sensing the discreet and sniffling progress of a hedgehog.

The sentence of the narrow road, bricks laid across from edge to edge, its rounded surface undulant. Bright moss growing in the seams. Pebbles and beechnuts pressed into the mortar dirt. The cadence of car tires, creaking and peaceful, a sound that swells until the bend, then coarsens and resumes.

MY PRIVATE NEDERLANDS. My language of confidential sections of my journal. Of the inner territory between world and word.

iii.

One afternoon, well into my Canadian life, I was riding my bike through a downtown intersection. On the opposite corner, a cluster of pedestrians waited to cross. Something large was on the road in front of them, against the gutter, blocking my path. A garbage bag. I swerved left to avoid it, and a young man in the small crowd yelled, "Pas op!" I looked over my left shoulder and saw that I'd moved in front of a speeding pickup truck, and when I swung back to the edge of the street, I felt the airstream as the vehicle's side-view mirror passed my head.

I was already a few blocks away, feeling foolish, lucky, and shaken, when I realized I'd been alerted in Dutch. Maybe by a tourist, or an exchange student, who in a moment of alarm had spewed the first words that came to mind. For which I happened to be wired, as it were, from ears to brain to palms gripping the ribbed handlebars.

MOTHER TONGUE, IS this how you come to your estranged ones, in wayward outbursts, sparing their lives?

NOT LONG AGO, a child named Nancy was interned at the Kamloops Indian Residential School. She was forgetting parts of her language. Not through the slow attrition of immigration but from the purposeful brutality of her teachers, and of their supervisors, and of their supervisors' supervisors, in a funnel of power under which a young girl, stolen from her parents, was a lonesome target. One evening, she recalls lying in bed: "I remembered trying to remember some words . . . I was trying to remember one word and that was *squirrel* and it was so easy . . . I remember struggling with it all day and trying to remember. And then at night when I went to bed, I kept thinking about it and thought and thought and then it came up—*dltg.*"[3]

Mother tongue, is this when you'll surface, under cover of night, in the mind's somnolent dark?

I ONCE WORKED on a hospital ward where an elderly woman lay in a catatonic state. She stayed in bed, refused to drink, eat, or speak, and kept her eyes fixed on the ceiling. Because there was nothing measurably wrong, the medical doctors had been confounded and transferred her to psychiatry. There was no known family. The nurses turned her stiff body in the bed. Sometimes they managed to feed her a spoonful of water or soup.

The woman had been brought to the hospital by her landlord, who described her as determined and self-reliant, a widowed Dutch immigrant. He said she hadn't answered her door for a day or two, and he found her sitting mute and immobile in a chair. I could picture that chair. Upholstered in dim florals, brown crocheted covers over the armrests. The carpet still scrolled with a vacuum's linear wake. The tick of a heavy, wooden clock.

I offered to speak Dutch to her. The staff agreed, and they gathered around her bed to observe. I stood beside the IV pole with its translucent bag of fluid and the nightstand where a small pink sponge on a stick sat in a Styrofoam cup of water. The woman was emaciated, her body dry as kindling under the sheets. I had the sense that a formidable will was at work. Perhaps she had made up her mind to die. I asked, in Dutch, *Mrs. P, can we do anything for you?*

The effect was abrupt. She snapped her head sideways and searched out my eyes in the group. Her gaze was bewildered, imploring, and furious. Holding it made me tremble. Then, only once, she shook her head conclusively. Turning away, she resumed her petrified state.

MOTHER TONGUE, WILL YOU come for your uprooted ones, when our souring, laboured breaths are numbered, will you be there to ferry us home?

NOTES

1. Yasemin Yildiz, *Beyond the Mother Tongue: The Postmonolingual Condition* (New York: Fordham University Press, 2011).
2. Ghita El Khayat, cited in "The Amazigh Adventures of Le Petit Prince," by Louis Werner, in *AramcoWorld*, Nov./Dec. 2017.
3. Celia Haig-Brown, *Resistance and Renewal: Surviving the Indian Residential School* (Vancouver: Arsenal Pulp Press, 1988).

Jónína Kirton

STANDING IN
THE DOORWAY

Walking I am listening. Suddenly all my ancestors are
behind me. Be still, they say. Watch and listen. You are the
result of the love of thousands.

—LINDA HOGAN

Many mixed-race children live in two worlds but may never feel fully welcomed into either world. Fred Wah, another mixed-race writer, recently spoke about this in an interview in *Maisonneuve*: "The advantage to standing in the doorway is that you can see both rooms, inside and out." Although the metaphor is apt, I can never fully enter either room. While "standing in the doorway," I have seen things that others do not, but for the most part I remained more an observer than an insider. I wondered how much not knowing the languages of my Icelandic grandmother and my Métis grandmother contributed to this feeling of being on the outside.

In one generation we lost both tongues, as neither my mother nor my father spoke the languages they grew up with. There was no mention of their ancestral languages either, which added to my confusion. Both sought to disappear all evidence of who they came from. Was this intentional? Was it their decision or that of their parents, both sets of whom struggled to survive in this colonized world?

My lived experience is mixed and yet my blood memory is strong. Despite being denied our language and our history, I always felt the pull of all my ancestors. I heard their calls and felt their need for healing. I am the doorway they enter and in a sense I am also a door. An unintentional gatekeeper opening and closing. Once conscious of my role, I began to listen more deeply for their gentle guidance. I became an opening, an invitation to another way. One made out of the weaving of both my father's Métis leanings and my mother's quirky Icelandic ways. Both hard-working folk who wanted to create a good life for their children, one better than the poverty they had grown up with.

I speak about this as one who was born in 1955, a time when status First Nations did not even have the right to vote in Canada unless they let go of their treaty status. As a mixed-blood Métis, I grew up within a family that was well assimilated. Given the prejudice against Indigenous people, at some point a decision was made to leave their language and culture behind. Most of them had a determined devotion to passing as French. Yet from a young age I knew to the very core of my small self that this was not true. However, it would be many years before I would fully understand what had been taken from me and why I was so certain of the truth of my ancestry.

At first, all I knew was that my little body loved the woods, that it was very brown and that inside I felt like I knew things that only a real "Indian" would know. I did not want to wear shoes, as I needed to feel the earth under my feet. I wanted my hair to be long and not styled, but my white mom wanted me to be like her, fashionable and put together. My "wild side" was a concern. From a young age it felt as if she wanted me to be a "good white woman" and was preparing me for marriage, but I wanted sovereignty and the woods. I knew I was different than her and her sisters who also loved fashion, who thought a good marriage was the best option for a girl. I most related to my Métis dad, who I resembled. He too loved to "dress up," as we called it in those days, but he had other sides to him. A complicated and humble man, he once appeared in local The Pas newspaper after bowling a perfect score. The title of the article was "Mystery Man," as he had snuck out after the game was over because he did not want the attention. It was not until I began my genealogy searches that I understood that he truly was a mysterious man, one with many secrets.

At fourteen, after spending the summer with my aunt Val in The Pas, where I met a number of people from the local reserve, I decided to confront my family. I started with my mom, who told me, "Yes, your dad is part-Native." She added, "He hates being Native," as if to caution me from asking him about it. She followed that up with something like, "Besides, it is not relevant because there is just one little *Indian* back there, so what difference does it make." Determined to know more, I went next to my grandma Rose and her sister, who we called Aunt Eva. Both of them shook uncontrollably as their bodies were overtaken with a fear that I had never seen or felt from them in the past. They both quickly blurted out denials. My grandma said, "No, no. We are French."

The shame they felt about their own ancestry followed them their entire lives. Both Grandma Rose and Aunt Eva were widowed at a young age and some family members say this is when they decided to say they were French—they feared that being single Indigenous mothers could result in their children being apprehended. Despite having been raised speaking Michif, they never spoke it again. There was another sister who continued to speak Michif, but when she spoke with Grandma Rose and Aunt Eva, they answered back in English. I may never know the full cost of this. What I do know is that, at sixty-one, Grandma Rose was committed to Brandon Mental Institute, where she received shock treatments and was heavily medicated due to what I was told was a "breakdown."

In her eighties, when Aunt Eva was ill in the hospital, she asked my cousin to hide the envelope containing her genealogy records. It was in the drawer beside her bed, and she was afraid the hospital staff would discover the truth about our ancestry.

A FEW YEARS before my father passed away, I told him I had learned from his cousin that his mother, Grandma Rose, and her sister, Aunt Eva, used to speak Michif.

"No. No," he said. "They were speaking French."

Was he lying to me or did he not know?

I persisted and continued to share what I was learning with him. Perhaps it was this and the timing of the Truth and Reconciliation findings that helped him understand that not only do we come from strong and resilient people but that our lineage was something to be proud of. Shortly before he passed away in 2017, at eighty-seven, he had made the decision to claim his Métis citizenship. This never came to pass, as he died before submitting the paperwork. Even so, I find comfort in knowing that the genealogy searches and the stories I shared with him about our Métis ancestors allowed him to begin to feel pride about our ancestry.

I HAVE WONDERED at times if it was these confusing messages about my own identity as a mixed-race woman that sent me into the arms of my first two husbands. Both were from immigrant families who were very rooted in their mother tongues and culture. My first husband, Paul, was German. His father had escaped from Cold War East Berlin. His mother was from West Berlin. My second husband,

Emilio, was an Italian who had played professional hockey in Italy. In both instances, my mothers-in-law were stay-at-home moms who preferred their mother tongues but spoke English well enough for us to converse. Both of my fathers-in-law worked in jobs that required them to be more fluent in English, but even so, I could always feel the hesitation whenever they spoke this language that was foreign to them. I could not help but notice how much more animated they were when speaking their own language, and even though I did not understand what they were saying, it was always delightful to watch and to listen to them. Unlike my family, they knew their language and their culture. They knew who they came from. They knew who they were.

Neither marriage lasted long. Both times I changed my last name when married and once divorced went back to my maiden name, Kirton, which I still carry to this day.

My last name, Kirton, is English. I am English, French, Scottish, Irish, Icelandic, and Cree, Ojibwe, Nakota, Sarci, Sekani, and who knows what else. There is little known about the histories of the Indigenous women in my lineage. Much more is available to me when it comes to the Icelanders. They document everything and do so much to maintain their culture, including restricting what you are allowed to name your children. My first name, Jónína, is on the list of acceptable names. I am named after my Icelandic grandmother, but for some reason my parents decided to name me one thing and call me another. They said it felt strange to call a baby Jónína, and my mom didn't believe in shortening names, so I had to go by my middle name, Lynn. Knowing what I know now, I am pretty sure they just didn't want me to have a foreign name, especially since my white mom was already being asked where she got me. When I reclaimed my name at thirty-three, I did not use the accents and decided to forgo the correct pronunciation, as I kept being mistaken for Spanish. It was easier to just say the J as one would in English, not Icelandic. By that time, I was so tired of being misidentified or asked what I was.

At forty I decided to try once again to sort out my ancestry. I used genealogy searches through the Saskatchewan Métis Nation, where my cousin was the enumerator. Our white mothers were sisters, and her very political Métis stepdad, Clarence Campeau, had been encouraging me to get my Métis citizenship. When I received written confirmation that my grandmother Rose (my father's mother) was indeed Métis, I wept.

It was some time before it became clear that my grandfather, Grandma Rose's husband, was also Métis (so much for the one-little-*Indian* theory). The French side of my family arrived in 1680 and moved across Canada, marrying locally. In my genealogy search I found lots of Indigenous folk, some who had signed half-breed treaties, and one three-time great-grandfather, Jean Baptiste Boucher, aka Waccan, a mixed blood (French and Cree) who had been Simon Fraser's interpreter and guide when he came to BC. Historical documentation states that he spoke many languages, Indigenous and non-Indigenous. One could safely assume that among those languages were French, English, Cree, Michif, Carrier, and Chinook, most of them the languages of commerce in the fur trade at that time. His role at Fort St. James is listed as "enforcer." My feelings about him and all in my lineage who had a role in the settling of Canada are complicated. My more romantic ideas about being Indigenous were shook, but it was too late now—I had to keep going. I had to understand why every time I heard someone speak Michif or Cree, I wanted to go sit on their knee. Yet if I try to speak Michif, my tongue becomes thick with fear.

It was Aunt Eva's daughter, Iona, who told me that when young, I used to sit on the knee of my fiddle-playing Métis grandfather and he would sing songs in Michif to me. My body remembered this. It would appear my body also remembered or inherited the fear of speaking my language. Or did someone chastise me for saying the words my great-grandfather must have taught me? I cannot recall but I do know that trauma lives on, even when we can't remember specifics.

Language lands deeply inside us. Perhaps it even lives on beyond us as the familiar feel of each word's vibration is passed on to our children, who may never have heard the language. Perhaps our bodies recognize it, just as they recognize the lands our ancestors come from. I know how my body hums when on the prairies, my homeland. Imagine my surprise on my first and only trip to Iceland, where I found my connection to those lands and that language.

It was 2017 and I had been invited to Iceland to read some of my poems, which were included in the *CV2* issue titled *Convergence/Samruni*. This issue explored the 140 years that followed the immigration of many Icelanders to Treaty 1 (Manitoba) and the impact on the local Indigenous communities. I believe I was the only contributor who was both Icelandic and Indigenous. The issue was produced in partnership with núna, an Icelandic arts organization that then hosted me and two other Canadian writers who were published in the issue. While there, I looked everywhere for the faces of my Icelandic relatives. I sat in coffee shops listening in to people speaking Icelandic. I watched body language, much of which I recognized from my Icelandic relatives. I have been told that my grandmother, Jónina, did speak Icelandic, but to my knowledge my mother did not. I don't know if I ever heard my grandmother or her siblings speak Icelandic. All I know is that wherever we visited I was hearing Icelandic words and they resonated throughout my body, opening pathways to revelations I am still unpacking to this day.

Our host took us on the Golden Circle Tour, which includes the site where some of *Game of Thrones* was filmed, Alþingi, the outside meeting place of the chieftains. Alþingi is the name for Parliament in Icelandic, and it has been anglicized as *Althingi* or *Althing*. Standing on those sacred grounds, I could almost hear the Icelandic words reverberating off the cliff walls. It was deeply humbling to know that my ancestors had once stood where I was standing, that they had not only endured but thrived on these starkly barren and pristine lands.

The following day, we were all invited to a dinner party at the home of a young Icelandic artist. When she answered the door, I was amazed by how much she looked like my grandmother. I had to hold back tears, as my grandmother was very dear to me and she had passed away just a few years earlier. Our host gave me a tour of her apartment, which was filled with artwork and family heirlooms. Seeing this, I felt a deep sense of sadness. My great-grandmother had come to Canada with nothing. The illegitimate child of a maid and the farmer she worked for, she was raised by her father, but was never fully claimed as family. I believe her immigration documents say she was their nanny. As the evening went on, I found myself wondering how different our lives would been had we had the continuity of language, culture, and grounding things like heirlooms.

AT SIXTY-FIVE I do regret not having learned either language but find myself without the bandwidth to do so. A difficult, trauma-filled life has left me with some memory deficits. Not only must I contend with the fear that I inherited from my Métis grandmother and her sister, Aunt Eva, but also a mind that cannot retain the words. Perhaps sustained exposure would help, but that is not an option at this time. These losses are like the dropped stitches when knitting a sweater. Yet, unlike a partially knit sweater, I cannot unravel the stitches and start over. I am where I am but take comfort in the knowledge that I have brought some healing to all my ancestors.

Visiting Iceland was the missing piece. While there, I had the opportunity to do a healing ritual with the cedar umbilical cord that my dear friend, Sharon Brass, an Ojibwe Elder, had gifted me with when she hosted a ceremony for fifty Indigenous Matriarchs in our community. During that ceremony she told us that we used to bury our umbilical cords, and I had always thought that one day I would return to Treaty 1, my Indigenous homeland, and bury it there. For many years I was not ready to let it go and brought it with me when presenting or reading—it helped me remember the sacredness of our teachings and the fifty Matriarchs who were in attendance. I wanted to remember to carry myself in a good way, just as they all did.

While in Iceland I thought often about the fact that Sharon's nation had nearly been wiped out by the smallpox the Icelanders had brought over 140 years ago, when they immigrated to Treaty 1. I longed for a way to make amends and when I got the nudge from my ancestors to bury my cedar umbilical cord in Iceland, on a black sand beach called Grótta Island Lighthouse, I was happy to comply. The beach had a peninsula that pointed toward Turtle Island. All these years later, burying the cord there, a place gesturing toward my homeland, meant the two sides within me could be united. My ancestors and Sharon's could now find some peace. It was a start, a step toward reconciliation.

AS PART SETTLER and part Indigenous, I can never claim innocence regarding colonization, the very thing that robbed us of our language and caused so much pain. My friendship with Sharon Brass and the way our stories weave together in such an unexpected way is evidence to me that we are not alone, that our ancestors are working behind the scenes to bring us the people and the stories we need, but only if we are listening. When I began this journey of reclaiming my culture, I had no idea it would take so long and I would have to be patient as each piece fell into place. I give thanks that even though I may never know my ancestral tongues, I have always had the continued support of my ancestors. They find wordless ways to guide me, offering pictures or scenes. Sometimes it is simply a feeling, to go one way and not another. And when they do speak to me, it usually comes as poetry, one line or phrase that I have to unpack.

At one time there were many voices, pushing their way into my awareness—restless souls seeking a sacred witness. At times the weight of this felt unbearable, but I am glad I stayed close to them and I know there has been healing because my ancestors have grown quieter. Their silence tells me they are satisfied with what I have been able to reclaim and understand about where and who I come from. Now we walk together, integrated and as whole as I can be without my languages. It is just as the Indigenous teaching suggests—that when we heal, we heal seven generations back and seven forward.

Eufemia Fantetti

FIVE STAGES OF LANGUAGE LOSS

DENIAL

A customer spots me working in the aisles of a chain mega-bookstore and scrutinizes my name badge. Her cobalt blue eyes remind me of the Adriatic and her hair is a shade of Cinderella blond. She offers an encouraging smile and pronounces my name correctly.

"Do you speak Italian?" The anticipation in her voice is palpable.

My suspicion: she wants to parlare, to practise la bella lingua. No doubt she knows the language, and now, deep in the labyrinth of a suburban mall, our fortunate meeting in the middle of this temple to consumerism will give her the opportunity. I almost hate to disappoint her. *Almost* is the operative word here. I've been through endless variations of this conversation and recognize what comes next, after my reply.

I return the smile. (Technically, the curve in my mouth indicates more of a smirk. At least my face doesn't contort into a grimace or a frown.) "I speak a dialect. My parents are Molisan."

"You must learn proper Italian," she admonishes in proper Italian. She lived in Italy for two years as a nanny and adored every.single. thing. about the place—the people, the pasta, the parlance. One day when her children are old enough, she plans a tour for the whole family of the bel paese.

The first expression that comes to mind is one my mother used to toss out with a scowl whenever she was annoyed with me: Beata te, Ma would scoff in a tone ripe with sarcasm, never meaning the religious, literal translation (Blessed are you) but an insult in lieu of benediction—Lucky you. I reply decisively in English, my poker face camouflaging annoyance and impatience: "I speak what's proper for me and my family."

Judgment envelopes the space between us. She would think my rural accent does a hatchet job on the lingua she loves; I am tired of pretending the exchange will provide any insight. I walk her over to a display rack of the novel she is searching for and hand her a copy.

Years before this encounter, steeped in humiliation over my poverty-drenched tongue (the second cousin once removed from standard Italian and closer to Neapolitan in lexicon and pronunciation), I tried learning the language in university. For a brief period, I sounded more articulate and educated. During a final oral exam in second year, I watched the professor's mouth perform phonetic gymnastics as he overenunciated vowels and masticated the consonants, correcting me for the third time. In his maw, the language that gave birth to opera morphed into a rhythm more aligned to a Texan drawl. My ego (or my pride) thought fuggetaboutit.

The classroom education wasn't simply a matter of learning vocabulary and conjugating verb tenses; the weekly lessons silenced the language that linked me to my parents and grandparents, and our shared lineage. Speaking the Queen's English version of Italian (Italy abolished the monarchy in 1946), I grappled with feeling pompous and pretentious. On visits home, I was a baroness putting on airs when I ditched the dialect, a member of the landed gentry fallen on hard times and staying with two temperamental farmers (my folks) with their clipped vowels and harsher consonants. My enunciation amplified the economics of the class system my parents escaped.

I can parley in formal Italian for a few minutes but am quickly caught out.

ANGER

In my biased opinion, our Molisan dialect is drenched in misogyny, patriarchy, paucity, and Catholicism.

My mother was a mentally ill teenager when my parents were catapulted into an arranged marriage. On their wedding night, she spoke some gibberish my father couldn't comprehend. Growing up, I talked with them in Italiese—the commingling of English and Italian spoken by Toronto's community of Canadese—a lingo my father labelled a "minestrone." This troubled wordy soup was the vocabulary of my mother's fury and the vernacular of my father's misery.

The push-pull for decades: I abhorred Molisan; I admired Molisan.

The dialect breathes through my entire being—elemental to my essence, my existence. Generations stood their ground in Southern Italy, surviving corrupt feudal landlords, earthquakes, disease, invasions, and war; predecessors whose mortal coils are knit together in my muscle and bone. I imagine their painful memories and joyful remembrances hidden deep in the chambers of my Molisan heart.

Dialects proliferate throughout Italy, and many older citizens are bilingual, able to communicate in regional and standard language. The first is considered by some to be more emotive, more expressive than the latter. So, attempting to learn legit Italian was a loaded affair—the romance over before sparks burst into a long-lasting flame.

Enter English stage left.

I started kindergarten unable to understand the teacher, and fellow second-generation kids translated for me. By Grade 2, I regularly begged permission to take elementary readers home with me, promising to return them the next day. I lay awake reading late into the night with my bedside lamp tucked under a blanket fortress so as not to tip off my parents.

After I discovered the beguiling world of books, my reading comprehension grew faster than my pronunciation skill. No one to check with, no one to correct me. *Thesaurus* sounded out as *the-saw-ruse*. *Maniacal* became *main-iackle*, rhyming with *shackle*. Combining the language I spoke and the one I could read resulted in haphazardly adding random syllables ("My favourite colour is purple-oh") and subtracting consonants ("Our class went to the liberry"). Mixing in the minestrone accent meant *sandwich* became *sangwitch* (I imagined a sea sorceress who sang to quell the stormy waves while my dad sliced homemade prosciutto).

In Grade 3, I was teased every day at lunchtime by the ginger-haired, freckle-faced boy seated next to me.

"Did you like your smelly sangwitch? Is it a good sangwitch? Because it smells terrible."

"You understood me." I hadn't called the bread ciabatta, or spoken of the sangwitch's delicious and aromatic contents: soppressata made by my father, a butcher, and scamorza, my favourite cheese. "There's no other word that sounds like saaandwhhhich that I mean." I spoke with my mouth open and full of chewed bits of salami and bread, elongating the vowels to prove I could pronounce the word.

He shook his head with all the weary what-is-this-world-coming-to weight a nine-year-old could summon.

This problem, my hodgepodge linguistic pattern, continues to the present day. I called a situation skewered, not skewed. I said my work wouldn't pass the mustard instead of muster. Once, I shared a worry with a friend that my anxiety and tendency to avoid attending events would turn me into a social piranha.

She corrected me. "Do you mean pariah?"

I paused. "Maybe. What the hell is a pariah?"

The dodge when people use words in English I don't understand is automatic—nod, closed-mouth grin, say "Right" or "Sure." I never betray that my internal dictionary is deficient. With friends, I am safe to ask for explanations, free to request the term or expression be repeated. Even now, I sound out words as a reader but never assume I've nailed inflection. Expanding my English glossary quenches a cavernous yearning I have to connect—linking terms to emotion, attaching phrases to thought, and anchoring sentences to experiences.

My facility with mispronunciations occurs in duet, in both English and Molisan. I scramble for words and jabber on until I find the one I need, throwing out English words with an Italianate syllabic flourish at the dartboard of possibility—the chance I'll bridge the linguistic divide between my dad and myself. This ridiculous method works 75 per cent of the time.

The other 25 per cent, my father loses his famous patience. "What you saying? You understanding youself? How can be you the writer and talks like a person who no make sense?"

BARGAINING

Before I was even a speck of a gleam in my father's eye, back when he was a boy of fifteen carrying an older man's concerns and burdens, my grandmother cautioned him not to name a daughter—should he be gifted one by God—after her.

The name was a mouthful and already old-fashioned at the turn of the twentieth century, when she was born. By 1950, when she voiced the opinion to her teenage son, the moniker was considered outdated—the equivalent of calling me Chastity or Prudence.

This life lived between two cultures (one faint and fading fast, like a fresco exposed to damp) brims with loss: I have never heard my true name spoken or whispered by a lover.

The last time one tried, the same outcome as always—my ears ached and my heart winced from the sound of the first vowel combination, the hardest for an Anglo-trained mouth to produce. All that could be heard was an injured werewolf's half-hearted howl at the full moon: *AaiOoooo*-femia. But constantly converting this Greek-word-adopted-by-the-Ancient-Romans handle into English leaves me depleted. More than the name feels lost in translation. Part of my identity is chipped away. For a while as a teenager, I introduced myself as Mia to avoid the anglicized version of my full name and carried this marred appellation into many McJobs; the sobriquet is still my make-a-reservation, place-an-order Starbucks name.

DEPRESSION

As a teenager, I imagined travelling the world with a steam trunk that would be stamped and stickered with the names of cities—Tokyo, Madrid, Paris, and Berlin.

I bought Spanish and German Berlitz phrasebooks and tried to teach myself rudimentary dialogue. But there was no one to converse with, and my enthusiasm flickered out.

I struggled with the drill-and-grill approach to learning French in high school and signed up for a six-week summer immersion in Chicoutimi. I arrived in the Saguenay region of Quebec eager to improve and thrilled to have escaped my violent home. At eighteen, I'd been studying the language since Grade 3, almost ten years. Even after all those hours in French class, I could merely carry on basic chit-chat. If asked to conjugate a regular verb or give basic feedback on the weather while walking along the Champs-Élysées: pas de problème.

In Chicoutimi, I wasn't allowed to parle anglais. Parfait, I thought. This was exactly what I needed.

On a phone call home, I tried to describe the bucolic surroundings to my father—the place was famous for its blueberry harvest—without using any English. Italian dialect mashed with low-level French ability in mind and mouth as I tried to tell him about my day. My dad didn't know French. He couldn't understand my garbled words, and the resulting discourse was disastrous, but I remained determined to succeed; I stopped, started, and mentally retraced my steps several times. Mid-conversation, I was hunched over and rubbing my right temple as I gripped the receiver.

"I went to the lac," I said, forgetting the word for lake (lago) in Italian. I used French, again hoping the word was a cognate that would smooth over my inability to switch between the two romance languages.

My father was confused. "U latte? You was go...for milk?"

This is what my dad heard next, shouted in Italian: "Be serious! How could I go to the milk? I didn't say the milk, I said the milk! Toronto is on Milk Ontario! We go for walks along the milk all the time!" I had a headache after hanging up.

One morning four weeks in, I woke up triumphant from a dream where I'd spoken French. I was jubilant. Unlike my classroom experiences back in Toronto, I valued being corrected by the instructor or by Josée, the woman I was billeted with; there was an atmosphere of encouragement that wiped out embarrassment over mistakes.

Returning to Grade 13 that fall, I was excited about my marked improvement until the instructor chastised my speech and oral presentations, demanding I use the French they spoke in France. I tried to argue (in French) that it was more likely I'd be communicating with someone from Montreal than from Paris, but after Madame ridiculed my picked-up pronunciation patterns, I stopped participating: pas de plaisir.

In acquiring French, I thought I could distance myself from everything I hated about being Italian: the brutal arguments, constant criticism, and heavily-adorned-in-golden-crucifixes damnation and hellfire of the whole kit and caboodle that I called home, but I walked away from français and considered the loss a personal fait-accompli-failure.

ACCEPTANCE

When I was twenty-five, my friend Luciano told me, "When you talk Italian, you sound like a sixty-five-year-old man seated outside a village cantina arguing with other geezers about the state of the world over a glass of wine." He marvelled at my Molisan and scrutinized my inflection as if it were a prehistoric beetle trapped in amber. I overheard him on the phone with a sister in Rome: "You wouldn't believe this unless you could hear her, but she's fluent in farmer-speak like the elderly from the Mezzogiorno."

In Molisan I say, "Ne capisce," instead of "Non ho capito," "che gehh" instead of "che cos'è," "Me fa male a cauch" instead of "Mi fa male la testa" if I'm among safe paesani. Rural peeps. Countryside kin.

In Molisan, my voice is peppered with exasperated sighs and resonates with exhaustion. My tone could be titled Tired of Dealing with Bullshit. The pitch is slightly deeper than my vocally fried English. Woe is imbued in idioms and articulation. At times, I sound more worried. The tenor, more frustrated. Some notes harmonize with an inherited "angling for a fight" attitude.

When I finally made it back to Italy after three and a half decades of avoiding the place (ground zero for our family's troubles), I stopped speaking around the city slickers in Rome—exhausted by the mocking that passed for teasing.

My friend (and unofficial tour guide) Nicoletta reprimanded me for my lack of formal address with strangers, and I bit my Canadian tongue.

But in Molise, every part of my body responded to the sounds and speech that have surrounded me for a lifetime, ever since I was a tiny being housed inside my mother's womb. My hands shook as

I stood in the doorway of my paternal grandparents' earthquake-damaged home and took pictures of the fissures in the walls angled like trapped lightning. My shoulders relaxed even after my cousin mentioned the village roads were deserted because of a viper spotted slithering along Via Rosello the morning of my return. A few times, I thumped my chest with my fist as if I had acid indigestion, solely to relieve the longing that made my heart ache.

In Colletorto, a neighbouring town seven kilometres from Bonefro (where my parents were born), I met my father's cousin Gina (who happens to be my mother's cousin too; my parents are related), and she is my mother's doppelgänger. I gasped when we met. In features, height, girth, gestures, and mannerisms, they could be twins. In personality, the two diverged. Gina was generous beyond measure, overfeeding me to the extreme, even for an Italian woman. She once slipped out quietly, leaving a table full of guests, to run into town and buy turcenélle (seasoned lamb intestine roasted on oregano stems and served on a stick)—the street food I hadn't eaten since childhood. I'd mentioned the delicacy wasn't available in Canada, and fifteen minutes later the mouth-watering offal was on my plate. In contrast, my mother's cruelty was incalculable—I'd cut off contact four years prior like a surgeon removing a malignant tumour. With Gina's family, I was immersed in bygone gossip at a fast clip and occasionally missed snippets of what was said.

Her son said, "You have a Bonefrani accent."

I stopped mid-sentence with one eyebrow raised. "Davvero?" There was a different accent between Colletorto and Bonefro? Was he kidding? Others confirmed it—I talked like someone raised seven kilometres away: a winding road scattered with emerald fields on either side and several rolling hills northwest of where I sat.

BACK IN THE Eternal City, full of piss and balsamic vinegar, I pushed back through writing when chatter embarrassed me. I retreated into silence, choosing not to confer if I didn't have to. This is what happens when one is served fear for breakfast, guilt for lunch, and shame for dinner and develops a hearty, genetically predisposed appetite for despair. I opened a notebook, drew the intricate lamp-posts of Amalfi, recorded details about the weather, reminded myself how fortunate and seemingly miraculous it was that both my paternal grandparents could read and write even though their closest-in-age siblings could not. A mystery my father can't explain either, in an era when literacy for Italians hovered at 40 per cent.

I imagine his parents—hungering for knowledge and thirsting for vocabulary—planting the seeds that led to the birth of a story-teller descendant fifty years later.

In the end, I wasn't in Bonefro long enough. Less than two days in total. My last afternoon there, a group of seniors swarmed me. One sun-wrinkled gent said he was my grandmother Femia's cousin and chuckled when my jaw went slack (she's been dead over forty years). A woman with a familiar face asked bluntly if I spoke to my mother (small-place scuttlebutt never gets old). One round-faced fellow who walked with a limp insisted on gifting me freshly picked plums.

"Portat' e ulange." He pressed a heavy bag into my hands. "Bentornato."

My voice cracked as I thanked him.

THIS PAST PANDEMIC year, my relationship with my father grew strained as we rummaged for words together to describe to his health care team the symptoms and side effects of his many illnesses and multiple meds.

Recently, he said, "Listen, this is important. I don't want you to spend a lot of money on my funeral."

I hollered that he was being ridiculous and pouring gasoline on my panic attacks. Then I hung up and sobbed.

My cousins also grasp Molisan and talk in the ancient tongue to their parents, but we use English with each other. We are not close: we meet only at burials. The words and all I hold dear will disappear one day, dissolve on the tip of the tongue like a sugar cube melting into espresso macchiato. So I press on in Molisan with my octogenarian dad while I still can. While the option is still available. Before my first love—the language that instilled affection for words and desire for connection—becomes part of a one-sided conversation at his gravesite.

Hege Anita Jakobsen Lepri

HOLDING MY TONGUE

Nuumte Oote, they call it—"true voice," but officially it's named Ayapa Zoque. It used to be the language of the village of Apaya in the Tabasco region of southern Mexico. It is but one of dozens of languages that continue to provide evidence of the Chontal Maya civilization, which was there long before the arrival of the Spaniards. In 2007, while working on a translation, I stumbled across the story of two brothers, the last two speakers of Nuumte Oote. It had no connection to the text I was translating, but that's one of the risks when you chase words—they transport you to unknown territory every day. All it takes is caving to a link in Google.

Manuel Segovia Jiménez and Isidro Velázquez Méndez were both in their seventies at the time. Instead of holding companionable conversations in their childhood tongue, the way I imagined older Mexican men would do, they didn't get along. They had no one else to speak their first language with, but preferred silence to putting their grudges aside. I imagined them, each outside his front door, waiting for the evening to sweep away the heat from their dusty village, with nothing to say to the other.

There is still much I don't grasp about languages, but one thing I do know: languages specialize in the natural world they're immersed in. Inuit and Sámi languages have an abundance of words for snow and ice conditions, so logic would suggest Ayapa Zoque has quite a few terms for heat, humidity, and road dust. With that vocabulary, the two men could have talked for hours without ever touching on contentious issues. The fact that they didn't meant their relationship really was broken.

I AM NOT a sentimental person. I take the daily flood of inspirational quotes, cat pictures, and saccharine stories in my newsfeed in true hipster stride: with a slightly raised eyebrow and tepid ironic distance. My kryptonite is language stories, stories about discovering languages, reports of language loss. So the story about Manuel and Isidro stirred something in me. I kept looking for more information. But beyond the initial BBC report, there wasn't much. I started imagining possible happy endings to the story: The brothers make up, shake hands, and by some miracle save their "true voice." I knew about the UN report that estimated one language disappears every two weeks across the world, but I also wanted to believe wondrous things could happen. Looking back, I'm not sure if it was the loss of language or of family that saddened me the most.

What I didn't consider was how all the other former speakers of Ayapa Zoque must have stopped speaking it while they were still alive, or died without ever passing their language on to their offspring. Manuel and Isidro may have stopped speaking to others, but they were the last pillars of the language, after everyone else had collapsed under the weight of Spanish. It takes a certain kind of stubbornness to stick with a program everyone else has abandoned. It is of no use to them—they speak Spanish to communicate with

family and friends. But is there something about Ayapa Zoque—
a sound, missing in Spanish, a cadence or a rhythm—that holds a
memory they can't let go of?

WHEN I WAS five, my grandmother came to live with us. During the
day, when my parents were away and my brother played with his
Matchbox cars, we would sometimes watch television together—
educational shows, because that was the only thing on during the
day back then. We didn't mind. It was our first television set, and
everything on it was still new and fresh, and full of opportunity.

"How are you?" The friendly lady inside the TV set smiled and sent
us encouraging looks. "Just keep trying, let your lips and tongues get
used to the sound of English," she said in Norwegian. There was a
brief silence, then a muddled noise. What came out of my grandmother's mouth resembled the syllables we just heard, but even to my
untrained ears, something was off. The vowels seemed to come from
the wrong place—somewhere too close to her lips. They had no depth.

Then I tried, and the tone was clear and effortless. It came from
a hidden space inside me: *How are you, how are you, how are you,* I
repeated. I sensed the vibration inside. I felt my tongue flip and curl.
My mouth had talents I never knew about, and I embraced this dis-
covery without worry.

My grandmother soon stopped trying to keep up with the mod-
ulations and the muscle strain that came with learning English.
Instead, she watched me learn the language, taking on the role of a
coach and fan club all in one. She'd tell me to listen up, to concentrate. And at the end of the program she'd tell me I had done well.
Later, when I was through level one and two of the *Start English*
series, she'd watch the reruns without me. I never caught her trying
to repeat the English sentences again, though. Her mouth was shut.
Whatever she was looking for, she hid in her heart.

I TOOK TO English the way a child takes to a secluded nook in the house. It became my secret place, my escape from the household rules. In English, secrets were allowed. In English, I could close the door without my mom barging in asking me what I was doing.

A WHILE AFTER reading the story of the Ayapa Zoque, I started writing down words my grandmother used but that had fallen out of my Norwegian vocabulary a long time ago. I wrote them down on yellow Post-its and put them in a pile on my cluttered desk. I can't remember how many there were—maybe half a dozen, maybe more—but the idea was that I'd type them up and save them for later. *Later*. That was the term I would use to mark some indefinite time in the future when my mother and I would get over the great rift from my last visit. That summer, she had taken to hurling the same words at my daughters that she used to hurl at me. I packed our bags and left within twenty-four hours, daughters in tow. *Later* didn't mean next summer, probably not even the summer after that. Some wounds take longer to heal.

In the meantime, I piled up words, wondering if I was making them up or if these were real terms I once used. *Sløg* was one, *begje* another. I had only a vague idea of what they meant—they came from a time before I knew dictionaries, and meaning appeared bit by bit. After a few months, I typed *sløg* into my search engine. To get a feel of its meaning, I tried to imagine my grandma's face when she said it. She didn't let her moods wreak havoc on her face. Her anger a slight tightening around her mouth, she muttered to herself as she watered the plants or did the dishes. When she was happy, there was a modest, almost coy smile. When she declared she was *sløg*, it would be with a slightly open mouth and widened eyes, barely perceptible behind her thick, big glasses. I held on to my grandmother's face for a moment, then hit Enter.

It turned out that someone had started a project collecting words from Norwegian dialects. Some *keener* from the western fjords, I thought, as most words turned out to be from the western part of the country. But *sløg* was there, only the definition was all wrong: *devious, sly*, it said. But what did they know, 1,200 kilometres down the coast from where my grandmother lived.

By this time, my mother and I were speaking again, though I was still unsure whether it was wise to return to her house. I called her, telling her I was trying to remember these words, trying to put together a list of words my grandmother used.

"What do you need them for?" she asked, her voice already on high alert. My mother has trust issues. She always worries I'm scheming to expose or trick her in some way. The fear is mutual. Probably there is some basis for this alarm on both sides.

I diverted her attention by telling her the definition I'd found online.

"Well, that is certainly wrong. We never used it like that."

We agreed that the definition was closer to that of surprise or shock, a little more negative than surprise and a little less strong than shock.

As I remember the conversation, I mentioned a couple of the other words from my list. But soon she started asking about what my daughters were doing and I tensed up again.

The next summer my father-in-law died in Italy. It was no time for trivial pursuits and useless research. Somehow my pile of Post-its got lost.

I REMEMBERED THIS WHEN, years later, I once again read about the last two speakers of the Ayapa Zoque language. In December 2011, Dr. Suslak, the linguist who was the source for the story, published a paper titled *Ayapan Echoes: Linguistic Persistence and Loss in Tabasco, Mexico*. It turns out there was no bad blood between the two men, whom Suslak calls Don Manuel and Don Chillo. Even language news can get its headlines fudged. One reason they don't speak to each other much is that they speak the language differently. Don Manuel teaches the language, a side activity to his production of religious souvenirs, while Don Chillo works as a cocoa farmer. In some instances, they use different words. They pronounce the words differently too. Dr. Suslak also uncovered a few more speakers of the language, two brothers who lived a bit farther away, and a cousin. The cousin's Ayapa Zoque is not very good, Don Manuel says. To compensate, she speaks it loudly.

One truth I've learned about languages: they change. As the words are bounced and squeezed and tested by new contacts, new experiences, a part of the experience remains attached to the words. I imagine the cocoa farmer refining his sentences to be as terse as possible, the syllables sharp, while the brother, proud of his intellectual skill and refined vocabulary, lets the words roll around in his mouth, embroiders his sentences.

ONE SUMMER, AFTER I'd resumed visiting my parents every year, my daughter made me aware of how I made tiny, creaky noises when my parents spoke English.

"It sounds like you want to correct them," she said, "or make a note of their errors for later. You sound like an asshole."

I recognized it as soon as she said it. I remember hearing these noises from somewhere (my nose? my throat?), thinking only I could hear them.

My parents grew up without a second language. By the time they learned to speak it, the deep grammar inside them was frozen in Norwegian mode, and no amount of training could keep them from making the same mistakes over and over. And when they're eager, they mix up their *v*'s and *w*'s, and my father will talk about the Wikings who travelled vest. Still, they master English well enough to converse easily about most topics, and since almost their entire brood married foreigners, they get to practise it almost daily.

By the next summer, I had let go of the noises. I would lock my jaw and push my tongue against the top of my mouth instead. My jaw hurt, but not a sound escaped. Not that this made me any less of an asshole.

I wonder if the last speakers of Ayapa Zoque made noises at the other's errors, or ground their teeth when they heard an odd pronunciation.

WHEN I WAS YOUNG, I spent years composing poetry that never got published. Eventually, I gave up writing and spent the next twenty years penning nothing but reports and grocery lists. Later, in my first introductory writing class, which I signed up for on a whim, we spent a great deal of time on the concept of "finding your voice." I felt such relief at finally opening up to writing again that I didn't pay much attention to my "voice," I just wrote. It was later, when people started asking me why I had decided to write in English, I began to wonder about my "true voice."

"Because I need an ocean and a language between my mother and me to feel safe enough to write," I reply most times.

"Because my life is so complicated, language-wise, that no single language covers it if I want to write about my own experience," I say when I'm with other translators.

"Because the language I grew up with was a dialect, and using standard Norwegian feels like a straitjacket," I insist to other Scandinavians.

Sometimes, when I'm alone and I find a hole in my English vocabulary or stumble over my words, I tell myself it's because I am a fraud and a fake. No real writer lets go of their first language.

MY MOTHER TONGUE is not dead. It is there on my laptop every day as I toil away on the week's translation. But my connection with it is looser; I no longer actively shape it to my needs; I google turns of phrase and choose what is most common.

Still, the thought of the Post-its with my grandmother's words, and how I lost them, remains a source of swift, irrational anger. It comes back to me as I'm cleaning my desk, ready to move my study to the third floor, now that my youngest daughter has moved out. There is a pile of paper at my feet, but I've hardly made a dent in the mountains still on the desktop. There are papers from when my daughters were in elementary school. I can't believe they weren't purged the last time I moved my office space. How is it possible that I've kept all this useless stuff, but lost the Post-its that I really cared about? I scatter another pile of miscellanea, as if throwing things around will make the sticky notes reappear. I swear loudly in Norwegian, using the worst words we have: *Fan i hælvete, Satans kuk*, mixing the many Norwegian names for the devil with rude names for male genitalia. The profanities burst off my tongue as if I had never stopped using them.

THE MOUTH IS its own geography of valleys and ridges, hollows and mounds. But unlike the landscapes outside, it is immensely flexible and can be adapted to our needs. The lips can be widened and tightened, tensed and relaxed, allowing us to smile, kiss, and produce the bilabial plosives /b/ and /p/.

The tongue is capable of bending and twisting, extending and retracting, and it lets us taste, suck, and pronounce /t/, /d/, /k/, /g/. The position of the tongue also alters the sound of vowels, allowing us to distinguish between an /e/ and an /æ/, or an /i/ and a /y/.

Phonetics provides us with terminology and *"mouth* maps" that describe with great accuracy how language sounds are produced. The opportunities are almost endless. We're equipped from birth to produce sounds from all over the map, but within our first ten to fifteen years of life, we learn to settle into the specific sounds that are prevalent in our own language, our mother tongue, and lose the ability to produce "foreign" sounds. The mouth adopts a *neutral* or resting position specific to that.

When I hear a new language for the first time, before I'm able to distinguish syllables and words, this is what I hear: sound shaped in unfamiliar spaces. Thai and Vietnamese sound like throat languages, with their glottal stops and tones. Spanish is a "lips and teeth" language, with strong *s* sounds and open vowels coming straight at us.

WHEN I FINALLY hear Ayapa Zoque spoken, I immediately classify it as more of a *throat and lower mouth* language than a *lips and teeth* language. As I explore the tiny corner of YouTube dedicated to the language, I can see how, even there, it is squeezed between heavy chunks of Spanish. Isidro and Manuel are interviewed in Spanish, and most interviewers are more interested in commentating than in listening.

My Spanish is good enough to follow the Spanish commentary, but when Isidro and Manuel speak it, I lose half of every sentence. It is Spanish—but some of the sounds are still stuck in Zoque. Isidro is missing quite a few teeth, making the Spanish sounds even harder to pronounce.

This is the face of language death: as Spanish advances, the Tabascan languages retreat. Soon they are seen as backward and embarrassing. As gradually fewer people speak them and children stop learning them, they become ever less useful. In the end, the last speakers die.

Yet, in a report from 2016, produced by a Mexican TV network, there is a group picture of Ayapa Zoque speakers and learners. Manuel and Isidro are both there, as is Manuel's son. I don't know who the others are, but they seem to have been part of the third annual fiesta dedicated to the language. There are other images of the town square filled with young girls in embroidered white dresses. There are dance performances, collective artworks. If Ayapa Zoque is on its deathbed, they are giving it one hell of a send-off.

ONE OF THE CHARACTERISTICS of the Senja dialect my grandmother spoke, like most Northern Norwegian dialects, is the use of palatalization—a sound change where certain combinations of sounds involving *n* or *l* are hugged by the tongue and held longer against the palate. The movement is the same you see in infants sucking milk. It is a sound you find in Northern Norway, and again in the Mediterranean. Spanish uses the double *ll* and the ñ to distinguish it from other consonants. Italian uses *gl* and *gn* to define it.

My favourite words all contain this sound, which has been censored out of the written Norwegian language. When I write *sommarvijnn* (summer breeze), *vainn* (water), and *sainnt* (true), I invent the spelling as I go. I pause regularly, to see if the letters look the way my tongue feels. As I push my tongue against the roof of my mouth, I remember things: the smell of salt on a windy day; the taste of a cloudberry not quite ripe; the texture of longing for things long lost.

ACKNOWLEDGEMENTS

FIRST AND FOREMOST, we are deeply grateful to Hazel Millar and Jay MillAr for believing in this project and giving it a home at Book*hug. Thank you for your enthusiastic interest, support, and endorsement. Our gratitude extends also to Stuart Ross for copy-editing and Ingrid Paulson for the type and design.

We are indebted to the writers and editors who shared their experiences and wisdom with us as we began to envision this book. We value the time and expertise of Elee Kraljii Gardiner, Jen Sook-fung Lee, Jane Silcott, Fiona Lam, and Susan Scott. Tamara Jong and Jagtar Kaur Atwal, thank you both for your early engagement and belief in this project. Thanks as well to Salma Saadi for the early conversations on the issue of grammar shaming. Additional bows of thanks to our friends and family and communities: we appreciated everyone who bolstered our spirits and kept the home fires blazing as we focused on this work.

We owe an enormous debt of gratitude to the contributors who joined us in this endeavour and, truthfully, made our jobs easier with their diligent efforts and explorations of this topic. Writers, we were humbled by your efforts and strove to match your generosity; thank you all for trusting us with your words.

SOME OF THE ESSAYS in this anthology were previously published:

"Tongue-Tied" by Kamal Al-Solaylee is an expanded version of a column that first appeared online as "Tongue-Tied: The Silent Struggle of Losing Your Native Language," *Sharp*, October 2019. Parts of the essay also appear in *Return: Why We Go Back to Where We Come From* (HarperCollins Canada, 2021).

"Finding My Voice" by Jagtar Kaur Atwal appeared in *New Quarterly* 142.

"Moedertaal" by Sadiqa de Meijer appeared in *alfabet/alphabet: a memoir of a first language* (Palimpsest Press, 2020). Used with permission. This essay also appeared in *Brick: A Literary Journal* 103.

"The Seven Grandfathers and Translations" by Ashley Hynd, appeared in *New Quarterly* 151.

"Dear English Language" by Camila Justino was published in GUTS in 2016 and reprinted in *Wherever I Find Myself: Stories by Canadian Immigrant Women*, edited by Miriam Matejov (Caitlin Press, 2017).

"Holding My Tongue" by Hege Jakobsen Lepri appeared in *New Quarterly* 151.

"Speak My Tongue" by Danny Ramadan appeared in *This Magazine*, July 2019.

"Love & Other Irregular Verbs" by Sigal Samuel appeared in *Room Magazine* 34.1 and was reprinted in the anthology *Making Room: Forty Years of Room Magazine*, edited by Meghan Bell (Caitlin Press, 2017).

BIOGRAPHIES

Editors

LEONARDA CARRANZA was raised in Tkaronto and born in El Salvador to a mixed-race family of Afro-Indigenous ancestry. She currently resides in Brampton, Ontario, part of the Treaty Lands and Territory of the Mississaugas of the Credit. She holds a PhD in social justice education from the University of Toronto. Her children's book, *Abuelita and Me*, will be published by Annick Press in 2022. She is the winner of *Briarpatch Magazine's* Writing in the Margins contest, was shortlisted for *PRISM International's* short forms contest, and won *Room's* 2018 short forms contest for her piece, "White Spaces Brown Bodies."

EUFEMIA FANTETTI is a graduate of the Writer's Studio and holds an MFA in creative writing from the University of Guelph. Her short fiction collection, *A Recipe for Disaster & Other Unlikely Tales of Love*, was runner-up for the Danuta Gleed Literary Award and winner of the Bressani Prize. Her writing has been nominated for the Creative Nonfiction Collective Readers' Choice Award and was listed as a notable essay in *The Best American Essay* series. *My Father, Fortune-Tellers & Me: A Memoir* was released in 2019. She teaches at Humber College and the University of Guelph–Humber and co-edits the *Humber Literary Review*.

AYELET TSABARI was born in Israel to a large family of Yemeni descent. She is the author of *The Art of Leaving*, finalist for the Hilary Weston Writer's Trust Prize, winner of the Canadian Jewish Literary Award for memoir, and an Apple Books and *Kirkus Review* Best Book of 2019. Her first book, *The Best Place on Earth*, won the Sami Rohr Prize for Jewish Literature and the Edward Lewis Wallant Award. The book was a *New York Times Book Review* Editors' Choice and has been published internationally. Her translations appeared in the *New Quarterly*, *Berlin Quarterly*, *Paper Brigade*, and *Mantis*. She teaches creative writing at the University of King's College MFA and at the MFA in creative writing at the University of Guelph.

Contributors

KAMAL AL-SOLAYLEE is the author of *Intolerable: A Memoir of Extremes*, winner of the 2013 Toronto Book Award and a finalist for CBC's Canada Reads and the Hilary Weston Writer's Trust Prize for Nonfiction. His second book, *Brown: What Being Brown in the World Today Means (to Everyone)* won the Shaughnessy Cohen Prize for Political Writing and was a finalist for the Governor General's Literary Award for Nonfiction. His third book of nonfiction, *Return: Why We Go Back to Where We Come From*, was recently published by HarperCollins Canada. He holds a PhD in English and is the Director of the School of Journalism, Writing and Media at the University of British Columbia.

JAGTAR KAUR ATWAL left the English Midlands to travel around the world and settle in the wilds of Canada, after settling in the not-so-wild

Cambridge, Ontario she picked up again and went on exploring life in Edinburgh, Scotland. You can find her work in the anthologies *Love Me True* and *Body and Soul*, on Invisible Publishing's blog, and in *Room, The New Quarterly,* and *Prairie Fire,* as a winner of their 2017 Creative Nonfiction Contest.

LOGAN BROECKAERT is a graduate of the University of Toronto's Creative Writing Program. Her essay collection, *Boyish,* was a finalist for the 2019 Marina Nemat Award for Creative Writing. Logan's work has appeared in *Room* and on the Invisiblog.

MELISSA BULL is a writer and translator based in Montreal. She is the editor of *Maisonneuve*'s "Writing from Quebec" column and the author of a collection of poetry, *Rue* (2015), and a collection of short stories, *The Knockoff Eclipse* (2018). Her fiction, non-fiction, interviews, translations, and poetry have also appeared in *Event, Nouveau Projet, Joyland, NewPoetry, subTerrain, Lemon Hound, Urbania,* the *Puritan,* and *Prism International.* Melissa is the translator of Nelly Arcan's collection *Burqa of Skin* (2014), Pascale Rafie's play *The Baklawa Recipe* (2018), and Marie-Sissi Labrèche's novel *Borderline* (2020). She has an MFA in creative writing from the University of British Columbia.

SADIQA DE MEIJER'S most recent books are *The Outer Wards* (Vehicule Press) and *alfabet/alphabet* (Palimpsest Press). Her poetry, essays, and short fiction have appeared in journals internationally and been awarded the CBC Poetry Prize, *Arc*'s Poem of the Year award, and other honours. She lives on unceded Anishinaabe and Haudenosaunee territory in Kingston.

REBECCA FISSEHA is the author of the novel *Daughters of Silence.* She writes fiction and non-fiction that explores the unique and universal aspects of the Ethiopian diaspora experience. Her stories, essays, and articles appear in various magazines and journals and in *Addis Ababa Noir*, a collection of stories by Ethiopian diaspora and local writers. Born in Addis Ababa, Ethiopia, Rebecca currently lives in Toronto.

SAHAR GOLSHAN 杜秀秀 گلشن سحر is a writer, language learner, and director of the short documentary KAR. She is an MFA candidate in creative writing at the University of Guelph, a former Diaspora Dialogues Long Form Mentorship program mentee, and a recipient of the Air Canada Short Film or Video Award.

JANET HONG is a writer and translator based in Vancouver. She was shortlisted for the 2019 JWC Emerging Writers Award for her book *Painted Windows*. She received the 2018 TA First Translation Prize and the 2018 LTI Korea Translation Award for her translation of Han Yujoo's *The Impossible Fairy Tale*, which was also a finalist for the 2018 PEN Translation Prize and the 2018 National Translation Award, and her translation of Keum Suk Gendry-Kim's *Grass* won the 2020 Harvey Award for Best International Book and the 2020 Krause Essay Prize. Her recent translations include Ha Seong-nan's *Bluebeard's First Wife* and Ancco's *Nineteen*.

ASHLEY HYND is a poet of mixed ancestry who lives on the Haldimand Tract and respects all her relations' relationships with the land. She was long-listed for the CBC Poetry Prize (2018 and 2019), and her work has appeared in several publications, including *ARC*, *Room*, *TNQ*, *Malahat Review*, *Changing the Face of Canadian Literature* (Guernica Editions), and *Best Canadian Poetry 2020* (Biblioasis). Ashley sits on the editorial board of *Canthius* and *Textile KW*. Her debut chapbook, *Entropy*, is available from Gap Riot Press. Follow her on Twitter: @ashley_hynd.

TASLIM JAFFER is a freelance writer and editor with a special interest in culture, identity, and home. As a first-generation Canadian parent, Taslim tries to pass down her Indian and East African heritage to her three children. Her bylines include *Maclean's*, *Huffington Post Canada*, CBC, and *WestCoast Families*. As panel moderator, keynote speaker, and radio show guest, Taslim brings important conversations to wide audiences about multiculturalism and belonging. She is currently pursuing an MFA in creative non-fiction and enjoys teaching writing classes in rehabilitative and community settings. Find her on Twitter @taslimjaffer and at www.taslimjaffer.com.

CAMILA JUSTINO has made Toronto her home for the past seven years. She is currently majoring in books and media at the University of Toronto with a double minor in medieval studies and Celtic studies. Since moving to Canada, Justino has dedicated herself to writing solely in English, her second language, which gives her the opportunity to understand the conflicted relationship with her mother tongue.

JÓNÍNA KIRTON is a Red River Métis/Icelandic poet, author, facilitator, and manuscript consultant. A graduate of Simon Fraser University's Writer's Studio, she received the 2016 Vancouver's Mayor's Arts Award for an Emerging Artist in the Literary Arts category. Her first collection of poetry, *page as bone ~ ink as blood*, was published in 2015 with Talonbooks. Her second book, *An Honest Woman*, again with Talonbooks, was a finalist in the 2017 Dorothy Livesay Poetry Prize. Her interest in the stories of her Métis and Icelandic ancestors is the common thread throughout much of her writing.

AMANDA LEDUC is a disabled writer and author of the novels *The Centaur's Wife* (Random House Canada), *The Miracles of Ordinary Men* (ECW Press), and the non-fiction book *Disfigured: On Fairy Tales, Disability,* *and Making Space* (Coach House Books). She has cerebral palsy and lives in Hamilton, Ontario, where she serves as the Communications and Development Coordinator for the Festival of Literary Diversity, Canada's first festival for diverse authors and stories.

HEGE A. JAKOBSEN LEPRI is a Norwegian-Canadian translator and writer. She had her first story published in English in 2013 and is still not sure what her "heart language" is. She's the winner of the inaugural Frances Thomas Memorial Flash Fiction Award. Her most recent work is featured or forthcoming in *This Magazine*, *Fiddlehead*, *New Quarterly*, *Round Table Literary Journal*, *Open: Journal of Arts and Letters*, *Carve Literary Magazine*, *The Maynard*, *Hobart*, *Agnes and True*, *Prism International*, and elsewhere. Find her at www.hegeajlepri.ca.

CARRIANNE LEUNG is a fiction writer and educator. Her debut novel, *The Wondrous Woo* (Inanna Publications), was shortlisted for the 2014 Toronto Book Awards. Her collection of linked stories, *That Time I Loved You*, was released in 2018 by HarperCollins and in 2019 in the US by Liveright Publishing. It received starred reviews from *Kirkus Reviews*, was named one of the Best Books of 2018 by CBC, awarded the Danuta Gleed Literary Award 2019, shortlisted for the Toronto Book Awards 2019, and long-listed for Canada Reads 2019. She is working on a new novel, *The After*.

KAREN McBRIDE is an Algonquin Anishnaabe writer from the Timiskaming First Nation in the territory that is now Quebec. She holds BA in music and English, as well as a BE from the University of Ottawa and an MA in creative writing from the University of Toronto. Her acclaimed debut novel, *Crow Winter*, was shortlisted for the 2020 Sunburst Award for Excellence in Canadian Literature of the Fantastic. Follow her on Instagram, Twitter, and Facebook @kmcbridewrites.

ROWAN McCANDLESS's writing has appeared in print and online journals such as *Fiddlehead, Malahat Review, Prairie Fire, Room, Skin Deep,* the *Nasiona,* and in the anthology *Black Writers Matter.* She is a member of *Fiddlehead*'s advisory board. In 2018, Rowan's short story "Castaways" was long-listed for the Journey Prize. In 2019, she won the Constance Rooke Creative Nonfiction Prize. In 2020, she received gold, as well as an honourable mention, at the National Magazine Awards—one-of-a-kind storytelling. Her memoir, *Persephone's Children* (Dundurn Press), will be launched in October 2021.

Born in Congo-Kinshasa, **TÉA MUTONJI** is a poet and fiction writer. Her debut collection, *Shut Up You're Pretty,* is the first title from Vivek Shraya's imprint, vs. Books. It was shortlisted for the Rogers Writers' Trust Fiction Prize (2019) and won the Edmund White Debut Fiction Award (2020) and the Trillium Book Award (2020). Mutonji lives and writes in Toronto.

ADAM POTTLE's books include the 2019 memoir *Voice* and the 2016 novella *The Bus.* His 2019 play *The Black Drum* is the world's first all-Deaf musical and was performed to the delight of audiences and critics in France and Toronto. His short story "The Rottweiler" was shortlisted for a National Magazine Award in 2020. He lives in Saskatoon.

DANNY RAMADAN is a Syrian-Canadian author, public speaker, and LGBTQ-refugees activist. His debut novel, *The Clothesline Swing,* won the Independent Publisher Book Award, the Canadian Authors Association's Award for Best Fiction, and was shortlisted for the Evergreen Award, Sunburst Award, and a Lambda Award. The novel is translated into French, German, and Hebrew. His children's book, *Salma the Syrian Chef,* was published in March 2020 to positive reviews. He is currently finalizing his next novel, *The Foghorn Echoes.*

Danny graduated with an MFA in creative writing from the University of British Columbia and lives in Vancouver with his husband, Matthew Ramadan.

SIGAL SAMUEL is an award-winning novelist and journalist. Currently a staff writer at *Vox*, she previously worked as religion editor at the *Atlantic*, opinion editor at the *Forward*, and associate editor at the *Daily Beast*. She earned her MFA in creative writing from the University of British Columbia. *The Mystics of Mile End*, her debut novel, the story of a dysfunctional family dealing with mysticism, madness, and mathematics in Montreal, was nominated for the International Dublin Literary Award and won the Canadian Jewish Literary Award and the Alberta Book Publishing Award. Originally from Montreal, Sigal now lives in Washington, DC.

KAI CHENG THOM is a writer, performer, and community worker based in tkaronto. She is the author of four award-winning books in various genres, including the novel *Fierce Femmes and Notorious Liars: A Dangerous Trans Girl's Confabulous Memoir* and the essay collection *I Hope We Choose Love*. She has published and spoken widely on the topics of mental health, trauma, trans rights, and transformative justice.

JENNY HEIJUN WILLS is the author of *Older Sister: Not Necessarily Related* (McClelland & Stewart, PRHC, 2019). It won the 2019 Hilary Weston Writers' Trust Prize for Non-Fiction and the 2020 Eileen McTavish Sykes Best First Book Prize. She teaches at the University of Winnipeg in Manitoba.

ESSAIS SERIES

DRAWING ON THE Old and Middle French definitions of *essai,* meaning first "trial" and then "attempt," and from which the English word "essay" emerges, the works in the Essais Series challenge traditional forms and styles of cultural enquiry. The Essais Series is committed to publishing works concerned with justice, equity, and diversity. It supports texts that draw on seemingly intractable questions, to ask them anew and to elaborate these questions. The books in the Essais Series are forms of vital generosity; they invite attention to a necessary reconsideration of culture, society, politics, and experience.

For more information and to order visit bookhugpress.ca

COLOPHON

Manufactured as the first edition of
Tongues: On Longing and Belonging through Language
in the fall of 2021 by Book*hug Press

Copy edited by Stuart Ross
Type + design by Ingrid Paulson

Printed in Canada

bookhugpress.ca